College Admissions

A PARENT'S GUIDE

Stuart White, PhD
A parent with a child accepted at Yale

Stuart White, PhD

Book Layout ©2017 BookDesignTemplates.com

College Admissions/ Stuart White. —1st ed.

ISBN 978-0999680520

Contents

Disclaimer

This book is intended for informational purposes only. The advice and strategies provided are to be used at the discernment of the reader and are not meant to guarantee results of any kind. The author has made every attempt to be thorough and accurate; however, ultimate responsibility for use of this material is the reader's. Legal, accounting or other professional assistance should be sought from a qualified professional.

Note on the Cover

Tour guides will tell you that if you rub the toe of Theodore Woolsey's statue in Yale's old campus, it will bring you luck and improve your chances for admission. In spite of her scientific bias, the day we toured the campus in June my daughter dutifully rubbed old Woolsey's big toe, yellowed over the decades from the countless hands of aspiring bulldogs. And low and behold, nine months later she was one of hundreds of high school seniors attending Yale's Bulldog Days for admitted students. Legend, luck or lottery? We will never know. But sometimes it just pays to go with the fiction and see where it takes you.

Introduction

Preparation for college begins in pre-school. Parents who take an active interest in a child's early development and a child who responds positively with a love of learning (especially reading), evidence of leadership among their peers coupled with sensitivity to their feelings, and a passionate commitment to something other than school will excel when it comes time to launch the college search in high school. For parents who wish this described them and their child but realize it doesn't, the college search is fraught with anxiety, confusion, and a feeling of necessity pulling them forward.

It is my hope that this text can help parents eliminate some of the confusion from the opening question they ask their child, "Where do you want to go to college?" to her final declarations, "I'm going to [*Insert School Name Here*]" and "Dad, start writing the checks." Defusing anxiety is beyond my pay grade.[1] And I can do nothing to reverse the necessity of going through the process in order to get to the other side.

Parents and their college-bound child will be bitterly disappointed if they are looking for rationality or logic in the college admissions process. To be sure, there is a semblance of logic. Applicants with a C average in high school and a barely passing SAT or ACT test will probably not get into Harvard, Princeton, Yale or any other elite college or university. But it is also true that valedictorians with an A average in a rigorous course load, with a 1600 on the new SAT or a 36 on the ACT and perfect scores on their SAT Subject Tests will get rejection letters from these schools. At the same time, some schools will

---

[1] Sarah Hecklau has tackled this challenge in her Master's Thesis, Everyone is Anxious: A Narrative for Admissions Professionals, Students, and Parents, on College Admissions and Anxiety
(http://scholarworks.uvm.edu/cgi/viewcontent.cgi?article=1666&context=graddis)

admit applicants using a paint by numbers approach where their high school GPA and standardized test scores qualify them for admission or they don't.

It is tempting for high school students and their parents to look for a sure-fire formula that will predict admissibility to colleges and universities, especially those schools that use a "holistic admissions" approach. They should plan on spending their days and nights wandering in the wilderness with little hope of finding it. I say this with all the certainty of a father who walked side by side with a daughter whose college search ended with acceptance by Yale.

Along the way, my daughter had to confront the reality that not everyone wanted her at their school or in their program. This experience of negation weighed on her naturally buoyant spirit and forced her to find her path to Yes in spite of the wound she felt. As a parent, I was angry that others in a position of power over her future didn't see what I saw. But the reality is that there are just too many qualified students who are as equally gifted as my daughter (if not more so) who are traveling the same paths as she.

At Carnegie Mellon undergraduate applications rose from 15,000 a few years ago to over 40,000 in 2017 for an undergraduate enrollment of about 6,500 students (16% admit rate). Their School of Computer Science applications numbered 6,750 from which they admitted about 360 (5% admit rate). In other words, for every applicant the School of Computer Science admitted, nineteen applicants were denied admission. Princeton University received more than 31,000 applications from over 10,274 high schools in 151 countries. It admitted about 6% of these applicants. Harvard received over 39,000 applications, the majority of which were from qualified applicants. The University of Michigan received 58,590 applications in 2016, its highest number ever.

At some point in the college search process, a student will hear something to the effect of "I am sorry to inform you that we were not able to admit you to [*fill in school name*] this year." Fortunately for most students applying to college every year, these will not be the final words they hear. Instead, their challenge and opportunity is to find their path to Yes and four years of learning that will open doors into the knowledge economy that awaits them.

The College Search

Do Your Research

Since I tend to be a bit obsessive, I spent a great deal of time in the fall of my daughter's junior year studying the college admissions process. I read a half dozen books about college admissions, colleges in general, where to find scholarships, and the whys and wherefores that you don't need an Ivy League education to get an excellent college education in the US[2].

I pushed my daughter to give me a list of colleges she was already thinking about and added to that list schools I thought would be good for her. I visited countless college and university websites on and off this list and read up on their admissions process, studied their student profile and of course took note of their cost.

At two websites, Cappex.com[3] and Parchment.com, I created user profiles that included my daughter's GPA, test scores and academic awards. This resulted in being flooded with college marketing materials but never any offers of scholarship. I was able to use these sites to gauge the likelihood of admissions for my daughter at schools she expressed an interest in or schools I thought she might benefit from based on her academic and extracurricular interests in high school. At one point I had identified 25 colleges and universities to research more thoroughly.

---

[2] Colleges That Change Lives: 40 Schools That Will Change the Way You Think About Colleges; Fiske Guide to Getting into the Right College; Fisk Guide to Colleges 2016; Ultimate Scholarship Book 2016; Where You Go Is Not Who You'll Be: An Antidote to the College Admissions Mania; Paying for College without Going Broke

[3] The founder of Cappex has written an ebook, *How to Make Colleges Want You*
http://www.collegepeas.com/wp-content/uploads/2011/12/How-to-Make-Colleges-Want-You-eBook.pdf

Collegedata.com contains comprehensive information on more than 2,000 four year colleges and universities. It gave me a quick and dirty profile of a school's student body, its cost of attendance, its academic and social life, and its history (see Appendix B). I found that its cost of attendance information was not always current. To determine the actual cost of a school, I had to find it on its website.

These three sites rely upon a college or university's **Common Data Set** for much of their information. This data set provides the most complete profile of a college or university you are likely to find anywhere apart from a school's own website. Parents and students who want to get a data-rich profile of the schools that interest them can google "Common Data Set [*Insert College Name*]."

The **Common Data Set** has 10 subsets of data:

A. General Information
B. Enrollment and Persistence
C. First-time, First-Year (Freshman) Admission
D. Transfer Admission
E. Academic Offerings and Policies
F. Student Life
G. Annual Expenses
H. Financial Aid
I. Instructional Faculty and Class Size
J. Degrees Conferred

In addition to diving into the data profile of each school I visited online, I perhaps became too enamored with the *US News and World Report*'s rankings of the nation's colleges and universities. Liberal arts colleges have their own ranking separate from public and private universities.

I paid attention to rankings because I wanted to get the most value for my education dollar, or so I told myself. In part it was an ego trip, which is what national rankings are designed to appeal to. I notice that I still puff up a bit when I tell friends that my daughter was accepted at Yale. It is alright to live a little vicariously through your child's achievement. After all, you will live through their down experiences as well, hopefully with empathy and shared pain.

To assess the value of my daughter's future education in terms of dollars and cents and not prestige, I also compared the return on investment for colleges and universities at payscale.com. More on this later.

What to Consider When Looking for a College

I think there are nine basic considerations that parents and their child should take into account when embarking on the college search process.

1. Academic Value
2. Core Curriculum
3. School's Core Competencies
4. Cost Coupled with Financial Aid
5. Location of the Campus
6. Campus Culture
7. Campus Safety
8. Study Abroad
9. Fit

Academic Value

Certainly, academic measures are key in looking for a college or university to attend. Measures like:

- student to faculty ratio,
- overall class sizes,
- strength of curriculum,
- time to complete a degree,
- accommodation of advanced placement college credit,
- faculty distinction, and
- noteworthy subject area, like math, computer science, musical arts,

all play a role in determining the academic value of a school. Given my daughter's experience with TAs teaching her advanced math classes at Michigan State University, she knew she wanted a smaller school. Since she values her relationship with her teachers in high school, she also knew she wanted a school where she would get to know and interact with tenured professors inside and outside the classroom. Fortunately, all of these factors are searchable and available using Google. Many of them can be found in the Common Data Set for the school you are exploring.

Core Curriculum

The schools we visited last summer with the exception of Amherst have a set of distribution requirements or a core academic curriculum that a student must complete in order to graduate. The typical core curriculum will include courses in quantitative reasoning, humanities, natural sciences, social sciences, language, and a mandatory writing course that cannot be waived regardless of your child's AP English scores. Apparently, colleges don't think that their students learn how to write in high school.

These curricula requirements are usually completed in the first three years of attendance. You should ask the registrar of the school you are looking at if there are any barriers to completing the school's core curriculum along with other degree requirements in four years.

A school's website and online course catalog will provide additional information about course requirements for graduation. You can also use a school's **Common Data Set** to identify the general areas of its core curriculum and record them on Appendix B. It is important to pay attention to a school's core curriculum since it will determine how much flexibility your child will have in scheduling classes for a major and electives or a dual major that interests her.

You should also determine whether advance placement credits and college course credits earned in high school can be used to satisfy core curriculum requirements. The answer to this question will help you calculate how many credits your child will need to graduate from the school they attend.

School's Core Competencies

High school seniors are now expected to know what subject they want to major in at college. Their college application will ask this since oftentimes the admission decision comes down to the department in which the applicant intends to major. For instance, my daughter applied to the University of Illinois School of Engineering with an intent to major in computer science. The University received 5,000 applications for its computer science department and accepted only 400 applicants. This is the same admission rate as MIT's overall admission rate. The University of Illinois' computer science program is ranked in the top five in the US.

When my daughter first embarked on her college search, she thought she would major in biology with an eye toward a career as a physician. She met with faculty in life sciences, including biology, at several colleges she visited in Michigan. Prior to traveling around the East and the Midwest, she changed her focus from biology and pre-med to computer science in combination with theater. Her interest in both of these subject areas led to the addition of Northwestern University and Carnegie Mellon to her list of schools she would visit.

Parents and their children can google college rankings by subject matter to identify top schools that correspond to their children's primary academic interests. Subject area rankings usually are based on core competencies at the graduate school level for public and private universities. You can find rankings by subject area for colleges that don't have graduate programs if you are diligent in searching the web. Alternatively, you can see what a school promotes as its core competencies. For example, Oberlin promotes its musical conservatory on its website and in its information sessions.

It is also common for a school's website to include videos or blogs of students talking about what their school means to them and why they chose to attend. Often, these commentaries will include a reference to the college's strength in math, or pre-med or public policy or theater arts, etc.

Cost and Financial Aid

The cost of attending college has become prohibitive, even if you are looking at an in-state public university. The in-state cost of attending the University of Michigan is about $160,000 over five years considering that many students don't graduate in four years.

There are a variety of ways to pay this bill: loans, scholarships, grants, work-study. Many students today are graduating with staggering debt. Low income students have access to Pell Grants but they don't cover the total cost of college[4]. Even students from low and moderate income families who also have access to need-based grants and scholarships are not free from debt.

Colleges and universities will have on their websites what is called a *Net Price Calculator*. This is a tool which the federal government has mandated. However, it is not always easy to find. Parents can use this calculator to get a rough estimate of what their *Expected Family Contribution* (EFC) will be for their child's tuition, room and board, books and personal expenses (Appendix G). This calculator **is not used** to determine an official offer of financial aid.

---

[4] In 2016, the maximum Pell Grant was $5,775

Parents should note that they cannot opt out of their financial responsibility for their child's education. Even if you refuse to pay any portion of your child's tuition, room and board, or other expenses, your *Expected Family Contribution*, as calculated by a school's financial aid office, will be used to determine whether your child receives financial aid or not.

To be considered for aid, a parent or your child needs to complete the Free Application for Federal Student Aid (FAFSA) in your child's senior year in high school. You will want to complete this application as soon as it opens up. Some schools dole out aid on a first come, first served basis and if you wait until spring to complete the FAFSA, your child may be eligible for aid but the school may not have it to give.

Some schools also require parents or applicants to complete the CSS/Financial Aid Profile. It delves deeper into a family's finances and includes assets like home equity that FAFSA does not. Be prepared to provide your federal tax returns if asked by the schools from which you are seeking aid.

Basically, the financial aid calculation will look at parental income and parental assets as well as the college applicant's. If a child has a trust, a savings or checking account, or other investments, the school will consider 20% of it as available for covering the cost of her education. In contrast, the school will only consider 5% of parental assets which includes stocks, bonds, cash, trusts, real estate equity, retirement funds, 529 accounts held in trust for a dependent child, and business equity as available for the cost of a college education. Each school uses its own formula so there is no clear-cut way to predict how much aid a family might receive for their child other than using each school's net price calculator.

There is in the world of college aid, the concept of need blind. This means that a school will look at an application and make a decision about admission without regard to the applicant's need for financial aid. However, many admissions experts claim that schools may look more favorably on students who will be paying their own way without the need for financial assistance[5].

---

[5] Dr. Kat Cohen. *10 College Admissions Secrets: An Insiders Look from an Elite College Counselor.* https://www.noodle.com/articles/10-college-admissions-secrets-from-an-ivy-league-counselor

Another thing to keep in mind is that some schools are solely need based when determining financial aid[6]. The only top ten universities in the country that offer merit aid are Duke, the University of Chicago and John Hopkins University. Most of the top liberal arts colleges are solely need based in their financial assistance[7]. This has driven middle class and upper middle class families with assets set aside for college and retirement to look outside the school financial aid office for scholarship assistance when considering colleges and universities with price tags exceeding $70,000 a year.

If an applicant is fortunate to get accepted at a top college or university, she may be the beneficiary of a generous financial aid policy that attempts to let students graduate debt free. For a family making less than $65,000 a year, with comparable assets, the student cost to attend a school like Harvard or Stanford is $0. A student from a family with a middle class income and modest assets can expect to pay Harvard what he or she would pay an in-state university to attend. It is not unheard of that a student whose family earns $200,000 and has hundreds of thousands of dollars in assets will still receive some financial aid at a top college or university.

The same family earning $200,000 should not expect to receive any financial assistance from a public university unless they have some special circumstances like a child with cancer who needs the family's assets for care. And even these families may not qualify for aid.

In the end financial aid is a negotiable item, if you meet the threshold for need. A college may rethink its offer of assistance if a student can show evidence of a competing college's more generous package. But you need to be mindful that with the rising cost of higher education, most financial assistance is need based with an eye first to the students on the bottom of the economic ladder.

One factor that is often overlooked when considering the cost of college education is the Return on Investment (ROI) associated with a

---

[6] *The Colleges that Offer No Merit Scholarships*
www.barbaraaustin.com/?p=388

[7] I created an Excel spreadsheet that listed all of the schools that were under consideration and included a column that indicated whether the school offered merit aid and another column with the deadline for applying if merit aid required a separate application from the college application. The spreadsheet listed 38 colleges or universities of which 21 provided merit aid. Most of these were public universities or second tier liberal arts colleges. Fifteen of the schools on this list were ranked in the top 20 universities and colleges in the US and only 5 offered merit aid.

given college or university. Payscale.com has a chart that compares the 20-year ROI of over 1,000 colleges and universities to their four year cost of attendance.

For instance, an in-state University of Michigan student can expect a $104,000 four year cost of attendance with a 20-year ROI of $667,000. Yale University in contrast would cost $243,000 over four years and return $643,000 in 20 years. On the basis of ROI alone, the University of Michigan is a better investment than Yale.

When looking at the cost of college, it also pays to look at the near term and long term value of its degree. The median salary of a graduate from Carnegie-Mellon's School of Computer Science was $109,000 in 2016, not including signing bonuses.

One cost consideration that is often overlooked is the cost of housing and board for students who don't live on campus. Not every college and university has the capacity to house its students all four years. Parents should ask both the financial aid office and the admissions office about a school's housing policy. If upperclassmen are required to live off campus, then a review of the surrounding housing options is advised. Both quality of housing and cost of housing should be taken into account. If a family assumes it will receive financial aid for four years, then the parents should inquire if this aid includes the cost of living off campus in the event the school cannot house all of its undergraduates for four years.

This consideration can be especially critical in urban environments where the cost of housing is beyond reason. For instance, a quick look at Zillow.com for apartments in Cambridge near Harvard shows that rents for a two-bedroom apartment are running between $2,000 and $3,500 a month. This may explain why 98% of its undergraduates live on campus all four years.

Rents near Northwestern University in Evanston and the University of Michigan in Ann Arbor are comparable to Cambridge. Neither U of M nor Northwestern can accommodate students in campus housing for all four years of undergraduate studies. Parents will need to calculate the likely off-campus housing costs for their children attending these schools in their junior and senior years in order to get a true estimate of the four-year college cost for U of M, Northwestern, or other schools with similar housing policies that preclude four year residency on campus.

Finally, most offers of financial aid will assume a student contribution. This amount can be earned through work-study jobs on campus or off campus work like waiting tables. If your child is receiving federal aid, then she will be eligible for federally funded work-study jobs. She should plan to apply for a work-study job as soon as her school opens applications for work-study jobs. Schools usually open applications during the summer. In any event, parents should have a plan for how their child is going to contribute to the cost of her education with earnings during the school year or summer recess.

Location, location, location

For many students in public schools, attending college will be the first time they spend any prolonged time away from home. This distance may represent a blessing or a challenge for both child and parents. Proximity to home will impact a student's ability to reconnect with his or her family. A student from the East Coast attending Stanford in Palo Alto, California will have a longer haul and greater cost to return home for holidays and school breaks than the same student going to schools in New York or Boston.

Another prime consideration is the community where a college or university is located. Does your child want to live in a rural, pastoral glade with an adjoining one-light town, two restaurants, one bar, a drug store and few rental properties for students who want to live off campus? Is she accustomed to living in an urban setting and wants the vitality and array of choices associated with a city like Boston, New York, Chicago or Los Angeles? Or does the middle of the road suburban environment of a school like Swarthmore, which is just outside Philadelphia, appeal to her? Your child probably won't know what community location appeals to her until she has had a chance to visit. Once my daughter was exposed to the languid setting of Oberlin and Kenyon, she was fairly certain neither would sustain her for four years. At the same time, the density and intensity of Cambridge just outside Boston held less appeal for her than the mid-size city of New Haven with its sheltered campus life.

What socio-political values does your child subscribe to? Is she a liberal dual coast type who will thrive in communities like Palo Alto and Berkeley on the west coast or New York City and Boston on the east coast? Is she an industrious, God fearing type who will find like-minded souls in the smaller towns of the Midwest? Is she an adventurer who sees the mountain communities of the Rockies as opportunities for excitement and personal challenge? Does she appreciate the continuity and gentility of the South with its tradition of hospitality and respect for tradition?

Finally, does your child want regional diversity or homogeneity? This consideration is more important than one might think at first. Most students attending large public universities reside in the school's home state. According their 2016 **Common Data Sets**, the proportion of in-state freshmen was

90% at University of Florida

86% at University of Illinois

84% at Michigan State University

83% at North Carolina Chapel Hill

61% at Purdue University

59% at University of Michigan–Ann Arbor

29% at Northwestern

19% at Kenyon

18% at Princeton

16% at Harvard

12% at Swarthmore

12% at Duke

12% at Carnegie Mellon

8% at Yale

7% at Oberlin

Liberal arts colleges and private universities are more likely to have fewer in-state residents in part because they seek diversity in their freshman class and don't have to answer to state legislatures appropriating money for the higher education of their constituents.

Another important consideration about location is the community ethos surrounding the school. Town and gown relationships matter.

The local community surrounding a college or university is not always hospitable. Likewise, colleges and universities can insulate themselves from the community influences beyond it. However, the knowledge economy has begun to reshape town and gown through the emergence of the business incubator phenomenon associated with the intellectual property that originates in the university or collegiate center and migrates outward to the local economy.

For instance, Carnegie Mellon wants to be an incubator of startups and technological innovation in the East the same way that the Silicon Valley is in the West. Pittsburg is noted for its innovation in robotics and now schools like Carnegie want to propel it even further into the knowledge economy with its emphasis on innovation in science and technology. In this way, Carnegie should be seen as more than an urban-based university. It sees itself as an engine of the local economy and as such its academic programming and strategic planning will include this vision.

Duke and the University of North Carolina at Chapel Hill have been making significant contributions to the knowledge economy for decades through the North Carolina Triangle. High-schoolers interested in entrepreneurship in technology may want to consider schools that are part of a local economy's incubation of startups. These schools include the University of Texas in Austin, any major university in Boston but assuredly MIT and Harvard, Stanford in the Silicon Valley of California along with the University of California in Berkeley, and Duke and UNC in North Carolina.

Indeed, it is rare that a world-class university regardless of its location doesn't consider intellectual transfer from campus to community as part of its mission today. During an information session put on by the admissions department, you might want to ask how it transfers its intellectual property beyond its borders. Any college or university that seeks to remain relevant in a knowledge economy should have an answer to this question.

The university response may involve an explanation of how it places its students in companies with a global reach such as Microsoft, Google, Amazon or Facebook. While these are important benefits that may adhere to students attending a university noted for its technological competency, the larger question remains: how does an institution of higher education engage with the world beyond its walls to assure that the richness of its intellectual capital is shared with the world?

Campus Culture

There is the story that a college tells about itself and there is the way that it is perceived by prospective students, current students, alumni, and the general public. For example, a major university in the Midwest prides itself on being a land grant university with a significant number of Noble Prize winners on its faculty, an abundance of National Merit Scholars in its student body, and a reach that is global where land management is concerned. For the rest of us, it is also known as a school that knows how to party with students who enjoy their malted beverages on a Saturday night in the frat house. Both pictures of the school are enduring and reflect the culture that an enrolled student can expect to find.

Generally, college/university alumni and current students are the best source of information about a school's culture. For sure there are now websites that provide some inkling of what student life is like at School XYZ. These include collegeconfidential.com, a bulletin board where parents and students can post questions and answers about the college they are interested in. Another website that lets its users post almost anything they can think to ask is quora.com. Quora has sections devoted to college life and college admissions[8]. As a parent with a child headed to Yale, I was particularly fascinated with the Quora discussion of Yale's Naked Run through the school's main library during finals week. It's not really what I hope for my daughter when I envision her at Yale.

Beyond students and alumni, there are websites that rank campus life factors like best dorms, best food, best party school, best Greek life. For example, if your child is looking for a school whose social life revolves around fraternities and sororities, she will want to know what proportion of students participate in Greek life. This information may be supplied in the school's **Common Data Set**. You can look on collegeconfidential.com and Quora.com for what students say about Greek life on their campuses. You can also use a number of websites that rank Greek life.

Schools are using social media more and more to promote themselves and recruit students. In addition to websites and blogs, schools

[8] On any given day you will find a high school student posting an abbreviated resume on Quora or College Confidential and asking if they are good enough to get into College XYZ. You will also find parents asking about the safety or party life of University XYZ.

create Facebook pages, Instagram, Twitter, and Youtube accounts. These social media platforms let the schools extend their culture through a virtual frame, while controlling their message.

A key feature of a campus' culture is the array of extracurricular activities, including student clubs, available to students. My daughter is an enthusiastic thespian. She would not consider a college or university if it did not have sufficient opportunities to perform outside of the school's formal theater program.

She is also the founder of a high school club that promotes access to a STEM education for females. She intends to pursue this advocacy in college. The lack of a club structure supporting females in STEM on the college campus would be a negative for her as well. For other students, the availability of intramural athletics or band may be a deciding factor in where they apply. College information sessions and campus tours will spend some time extolling the depth and breadth of clubs and other extracurriculars that are available on campus in order to impress upon prospective students the options for release from the stresses of academics.

The **Common Data Set** collects information about a core set of activities at each college and university. This list in not intended to be exhaustive, but it does cover many of the basic interests of students like theater, dance, music, radio/tv/film, literary activities, student government, and organizations for international students, (Appendix B). The **Common Data Set** doesn't go into any detail about these activities; it merely provides a check box for schools to indicate whether they have them on campus. As such it provides a framework for seeing if the activities that interest a student are offered before visiting a school's website or visiting the school itself for more information. For example, a talented cellist may want to know if the school she wants to attend has a symphony orchestra before she spends time and money visiting it. The **Common Data Set** will provide this information.

Campus Safety

Campus security is a top issue with parents according to a recent survey of college parents. As a father with a teenage daughter, I too regard her safety as one of my primary concerns with the school she attends. When we toured college campuses, I always asked about the safety system the school had in place and what options students had at night when they needed to get back to their dorm.

Parents are understandably mindful about their child's safety on and off campus. This issue is so concerning that the US Department of Education has devoted an entire website to campus safety and security where a parent or student can check the crime statistics for a single school or create a custom comparison of several schools.

Collegefactual.com will also provide a rating of a campus' safety under its student life heading. You have to create a profile on the website to access this information.

Yale has an overall D+ grade. Needless to say, this rating doesn't fill me with confidence. Nor does it reassure me that the campus safety rating for the University of Michigan is a D+ or that Duke University's campus safety grade is a D-.

It may be the case that students can't avoid hazard wherever they go. But they can at least be aware of the level of risk and act accordingly. For a young woman attending college in urban environments, taking a self-defense course may be one way to prepare for living in a less than ideal environment from a safety point of view.

Study Abroad

Colleges usually will emphasize in their marketing efforts the opportunity to study abroad. Schools will promote this feature to prospective students in their information sessions, their published materials, their website and even on a campus tour. Colleges like Kalamazoo College promote it just as vigorously with their enrolled students inasmuch as studying abroad is an intrinsic part of their culture.

When admissions officials talk in their information session about their study abroad programs, especially ones that last a year, parents should inquire about the school their children will be studying at abroad. If you are paying for an education at Stanford and paying the cost for Stanford, then the foreign school where Stanford sends its students in Europe, South America, Asia or Africa should at least measure up to Stanford's quality.

Parents will also want to know what expenses the school covers when a student goes abroad to study and what costs the student and his or her family must assume in addition to the college's tuition and room and board. Travel costs can add several thousands of dollars to the parent's college bill if the school doesn't pay this expense.

Fit

Fit is one those ineffable qualities that can't be quantified. Your child will know it when she feels like she belongs. Certainly there are factors that are somewhat objective in this area. If the student profile is well beyond your child's capacity to perform, it will be a struggle for her to keep up her studies. If the school's social life revolves around the Greek system and your child likes to stay home on the weekend and read and maybe spend some quality time with a few close friends, the school's primary social dynamic may leave her feeling isolated and lonely. If the school is located in Maine with harsh, long winters and your child loves the beaches of sunny Southern California, Maine's winter climate may result in depression.

But generally, fit is a more inchoate and intangible thing. It is almost impossible to gauge whether one fits into a culture and an environment without being there to experience it firsthand. That is why school visits as an applicant and again as an admitted student are so important. It is also why your child should make every effort to know herself and what she wants from her college experience in the time she has to explore the college application process.

Fit really is the whole that emerges from the first seven areas of consideration in this section. If your child finds that any of these seven areas results in a feeling of unease toward a school, then this should be a warning sign that the school may not be a good fit.

The College Resume

Before your child embarks on her search for the college or university where she will spend the next four to six years of her life, she should prepare a resume that sums up the qualities of her leadership and leverage. The resume foreshadows the application. It will include an account of her academic accomplishments and a description of her extracurricular activities with an emphasis on those in which she has a leadership role.

Leadership does not just mean president or head. Rather it includes those roles that are needed to keep an activity viable. To be sure school newspapers need editors, but they also need talented writers who write monthly opinion columns or cover their schools' sporting events. Not everyone can be a team captain on the school football team, but teams need outstanding blockers, runners and receivers to win their games. If you've founded a club that has raised and donated tens of thousands of dollars to refugee relief, wonderful. But being a member of a club that donated 100 hours of volunteer time to flood relief in the club's hometown is noteworthy as well. The important thing is to look for and list on a resume those activities that show character, depth of commitment and passion.

If you have something in your life that makes you stand out from the crowd, showcase this as well. Mike Moyer, in his book *How to Make Colleges Want You*, calls this an NTA — a non-teenager activity. It is often difficult for accomplished adolescents to realize that there are thousands of valedictorians in the nation's secondary school system, thousands of captains of sporting teams, tens of thousands of students with perfect GPAs, tens of thousands of club presidents. And most of these accomplished students are applying to the top colleges in the country that have maybe two or three openings for every 100 teenagers who have evidenced leadership while in high school. That is why it is important for your child to identify what makes her different from her peers.

In my daughter's case, it wasn't that she founded a club to promote females in STEM that made her stand out. She went further and became a passionate advocate for computer science education in the nation's K-12 school system. She engaged in lobbying activities at the White House, on Capitol Hill in Washington, with the nation's Governors at their summer conference and with the Governor of her home state. She organized public testimony and presented it along with two of her club mates to the State Board of Education. And she pushed her own school to agree finally to hire a computer science teacher and offer a full complement of computer science courses in her school's curriculum. These are not the usual activities of a high school student. They showcased a kind of leadership that one associates with adults trying to influence public policy and obviously made enough of an impact with most of the schools she applied to for them to admit her.

The components of leverage include your child's academic record, her standardized test scores, and those areas where she loves to learn. Grade point averages and SAT Test scores are straightforward. A demonstrated love of learning requires a little more explanation. Does she love math? Perhaps she has a love of coding and has developed several websites for clubs and even businesses that have paid her for her skills. Has she mastered an instrument and performed regularly with a band, orchestra or symphony? Here is another chance to identify what your child has mastered inside the classroom and beyond that helps differentiate her.

The resume will give your child the foundation for a review of colleges and universities as she looks for ones to delve deeper into. She will use it when she visits colleges and asks questions of its admissions officials, student tour guides and even faculty. It will help her respond to the writing requirements of the common application, including the dreaded essay. It will also provide focus and context for the anxiety producing college interview.

My daughter created a resume early in her junior year and kept it updated as she expanded on her activities or completed steps toward her application such as taking a standardized test. A sample resume format is attached in Appendix A.

The Importance of the Guidance Counselor

My interaction with my daughter's college search really began in her freshman year. At my insistence, the two of us met with her guidance counselor to begin to chart a trajectory to her course work that would be college ready. If you haven't met with your child's guidance counselor, you may want to consider making an appointment and sitting down with him or her so s(he) can see that you are engaged and interested parents who are going to be monitoring your child's progress through high school with an eye toward college admission.

Making this connection is important because one of the letters of recommendation that colleges and universities require will come from an applicant's guidance counselor. Don't be surprised if the counselor is dismissive at first. Your child may be one of hundreds of students she is responsible for guiding. With repeated meetings, he or she will begin to take you seriously and help you and your child toward your goal. In our case, we needed the guidance counselor to intervene with Michigan State University first when my daughter was enrolled as a high school freshman in the University's gifted student program and again when she dual enrolled in MSU courses. It shouldn't be a surprise to learn how difficult university bureaucracies can be when you are just trying to get your child enrolled or your bill paid accurately.

You might want to consider hiring a private college counselor. Generally, you should look for someone who has had experience as a professional college admissions counselor or dean of admissions. We hired a retired dean of admissions at a medical school. He gave us a basic introduction to the college admissions process with some handouts that mostly consisted of links to websites where we could follow up for more information. Our session lasted about an hour and cost $200. He followed up with a review of my daughter's resume after she prepared one. Additional services like reviewing her essay would have cost more.

The advantage of hiring a counselor was in validating what I had already learned about the process and especially in letting my daughter hear from someone other than her Dad what she needed to do to prepare her college applications. Parents can spend upwards to six figures hiring counselors who promise to get their children into an Ivy League school.

Admissions Metrics

It makes little sense to waste time pursuing an interest in a college or university for which one isn't qualified. High-schoolers looking to make the most of their college search and their submitted applications will do more for their futures if they attempt to align their academic metrics and extracurricular activities with college profiles where they are at least in the mean. These profiles can usually be found in the admissions section of a college or university website. They are also accessible through websites like collegedata.com and the **Common Data Set** of the school to which the student wants to apply. The threshold of qualification for most colleges and universities includes a student's Grade Point Average (GPA) in a college preparatory curriculum and standardized test results.

Appendix C allows you to compare your child's basic metrics to those of a college or university in which she has shown an interest. The data for the school can be found in Section C of the **Common Data Set** for the school of interest.

GPA and Academic Rigor

An applicant's grades "can account for 75% of the typical admission decision." The more difficult it is to gain admission to a school, the more important an applicant's high school GPA and academic rigor become.

When parents begin exploring the collegiate landscape, they will discover that a significant piece of a school's admission criteria will be an applicant's Grade Point Average (GPA) — both weighted and un-weighted. They can compare the GPA profile of admitted students to their child's GPA to look for an academic fit between child and school. For instance, the average GPA for applicants at the University of Michigan is 3.73 un-weighted and 4.12 weighted, and the average GPA at Michigan State University is 3.5 un-weighted and 3.76 weighted. Assuming a rigorous course schedule, an applicant with a GPA at or above U of M's or MSU's average GPA will usually get past the first cut in the application review process.

The rigor of a student's classes in high school is also a key determinative factor in college admissions. A rigorous schedule of classes will include honors, AP and college courses. The number of AP classes will vary depending on a number of factors. Does your child's high school offer pre-AP classes that must be completed before enrolling in an AP class? Are the AP classes bunched together in the same hours of the day making it difficult for a student to take more than 3 or 4 a semester? The recommendation that the guidance counselor writes will include an explanation of the school's approach to honors and AP classes.

Supposedly admissions officials don't look at an application with a set number of AP classes in mind to determine whether a student is committed to a rigorous schedule. Instead, they will look to see whether a student has pushed herself with what the school has to offer. At my daughter's high school, students could only take AP classes in hours 3, 4, and 5. This arrangement limited the number of AP classes a student could take over four years to a maximum of 12 assuming the student took no pre-AP classes. Generally, students with rigorous schedules at her school took between 7 and 9 AP classes.

By the time my daughter graduated she had completed:

- Four years of English and Math in two years at Michigan State University's gifted student program,
- Eight Advance Placement (AP) classes in Spanish, European History, BC Calculus, Biology and Physics 1, 2 and C, and
- Two college courses in multivariable calculus and differential equations.

Taking a rigorous curriculum has its advantages. Depending on the school your child eventually attends, she may be eligible for college credit for some of her AP courses and her college courses she completes in high school.

One caution about dual enrollment in a community college course or college course while in high school: If the course is used to fulfill the high school's graduation requirements, a college usually will not apply the course for credit when the high-schooler enrolls in college. If the course shows up on the high school transcript, a college will default to the assumption that it was required for graduation. As a result, you will need an affirmative statement from your high school guidance counselor that your child's dual enrolled courses were not applied toward the school's graduation requirements (another reason for developing a working relationship with your child's guidance counselor).

One question students invariably will ask is, "How do I explain the poor grades on my high school transcript?" Not every high school student will have an un-weighted 4.0 GPA with eight AP courses and two college courses to their credit.

If your child has a legitimate reason for a significant variance in grades from one year to another, she can use the additional information section of the college application to explain why her grades are so different. Alternatively, she can ask her guidance counselor to include an explanation in his or her recommendation for why your child's grades varied from year to year.

However, if poor study habits or a basic indifference to school led to a variance in GPA, your child probably should own this reversal of fortune and target her search to colleges/universities where her GPA falls within the mean.

In other words, your child may want to attend Harvard. But if her GPA places her among the one-tenth of one percent of students admitted to Harvard with the same GPA as hers, she should be prepared to accept Harvard as a reach for the stars. She would be well served to look for colleges/universities where 50% of the prior year admitted students had the same GPA as she has.

Standardized Reasoning Tests

Another metric that most colleges and universities will look at is an applicant's standardized reasoning test scores. There are two tests that are offered: the ACT and the SAT. They are offered throughout the school year and into the summer. There is a fee to take the test which can be waived in cases of economic hardship.

In addition to the SAT or ACT, high school students take the PSAT early in their junior year. The PSAT is used as a predictor of sorts on the SAT, which is usually taken in the spring of one's junior year.

The PSAT is also used to determine qualification for National Merit Semi-Finalist status. To be a National Merit Semi-Finalist a student will need to attain a PSAT score in their junior year that places them in the top 1% of all test takers. Each state has its own base score from which semi-finalists are selected. National Merit Finalist status requires an additional step that includes an application above and beyond one's test result.

Both the SAT and ACT can be taken multiple times. Since they are tests that measure reasoning and mathematical abilities and not subject matter tests that assess mastery of a subject area like European History, there is probably a limit on how much one can improve from one test to the next, unless there are special circumstances like illness that would result in a sub-par performance.

In your travel around the web looking for information about college, you will find numerous websites offering test prep courses promising to increase your child's score by 200 points for the SAT and 2 to 4 points for the ACT. Parents can spend thousands of dollars on these courses on the one hand or let their child just wing it on the other. My daughter bought a test prep book and practiced for the tests by herself. She took the SAT once and the ACT several times with virtually no change in result. I doubt that a $2,000 test prep course would have made much difference.

My daughter doesn't test well on standardized reasoning tests. The pressure of time limits and the consequences of the result tend to stress her out. She does much better on subject matter tests like the SAT Subject Tests and Advance Placement tests. Still, she managed to achieve a score of 32 on her ACT test and 1470 on the SAT. This placed her among the 98th percentile of all test takers but that meant she was one of more than 75,000 test takers out of 1.6 million. This score placed her in the middle or at the bottom of applicants for the top schools to which she applied.

A high-schooler will eventually need to decide what standardized test to take. My daughter started with the ACT since it tends to be more knowledge based than the SAT. Recent changes in the SAT Test have moved it in the direction of testing knowledge.

Your child's high school may require juniors to take a standardized test during the school year. This test will in all likelihood be paid for by the school. In this case, you may want to just go with the test your child takes at her high school and decide after you see the results whether she should retake it or not. If your child anticipates submitting an application to a top school, she should make certain the SAT or ACT test administered at her high school includes the writing portion.

A few more things about standardized test scores. Some colleges and universities do what is called Super Scoring. This means they take the high scores from multiple tests and calculate a final, high score for an applicant. The ACT has four components — English, Reading, Math, and Science in addition to the composite score and the SAT now has two components — Evidence-Based Reading and Writing and Math as well as a composite score.

You can generally discover a college or university's policy toward super scoring on its website under their admissions section. If this information isn't readily found, applicants can always google — "Does *NAME OF COLLEGE* super score the *TEST NAME*?" If the school super scores and your child has taken the ACT or SAT multiple times with different results, then you should submit multiple scores as long as they will produce a higher score than any individual test result. If the school doesn't super score, then only submit the highest composite score of either the ACT or SAT tests your child has taken, unless the school requires you to submit all test scores.

Schools like Yale and Stanford require their applicants to submit all of the scores of all of the ACT and SAT tests they take in high school. In this case applicants don't have an option of what scores to send. But this requirement, which can be costly, doesn't seem to be that widespread.

Another thing to be aware of is whether a college or university requires the writing portion of the ACT or the optional essay of the SAT. These are separate tests that require an additional fee. When applicants apply for the ACT or SAT test, they will need to also apply for the writing section.

Prepscholar.com has a list of colleges that require or recommend the writing portion of the ACT or SAT Test. If a college says it recommends something, I have always read this to mean required. You can also find this information on a school's website or you can google whether or not a school requires or recommends the SAT or ACT writing test.

There is an emerging trend of colleges and some universities away from requiring standardized tests as part of the college application. A list of some of these colleges and universities is available at niche.com.

Finally, when my daughter and I were touring the East Coast and Midwest looking at colleges, we met with admissions officers who told us that they based their merit aid on a student's standardized test scores. For instance, schools like Albion and Kenyon offer merit aid and they look at standardized scores when determining who gets aid and how much they get. Also keep in mind that schools offering merit aid are interested in recruiting National Merit Scholarship Finalists. They typically award a scholarship in addition to the $2,500 that a finalist receives. To be a finalist, you must first qualify through your PSAT score. So there can definitely be an economic benefit attached to high test scores on the PSAT, SAT and ACT tests.

Standardized Subject Matter Tests

The College Board, which administers the SAT test, also administers SAT Subject Tests. My daughter took these along with AP tests.

SAT Subject Tests are typically required of more elite colleges and universities and not public universities. The University of Michigan does not require or recommend subject tests unless a child has been home schooled.

By the end of her junior year, my daughter had taken five Advance Placement Exams (AP Exams) and scored 4s and 5s, which will gain her college credit at most schools. However, the top schools to which she has applied are fairly stingy with college credit for AP exams and usually require a perfect score of 5 when they do give it.

AP exam results are not required for admission. Depending on the test score, they may be used to determine what courses to take once an applicant is admitted to a college or university.

It may be possible to cut out a full year or more if a student takes 6 to 8 AP Courses and scores 4s and 5s. In fact, my daughter would enter Michigan State University with enough credits to qualify as a sophomore if she chose to go there. As it is she will be attending Yale, which is very miserly when it comes to awarding credit for AP test results. They give no credit for college courses taken in high school. Their view appears to be that everyone who applies and is admitted will have a slew of AP and college courses under their belt or they wouldn't be admitted in the first place. So there is no reason to reward applicants for what is the expected high school curriculum.

You have to be careful about calculating prospective college credit from AP Tests and dual enrolled college courses. Some schools limit the number of AP and college credits earned in high school that they will allow a student to apply toward graduation. And most schools will not let a student use advanced standing credits to place-out-of-core curriculum requirements.

The AP courses will also factor into a student's GPA. Students have both an un-weighted and a weighted GPA. In my daughter's case, her un-weighted GPA is a 4.0 and her weighted GPA is a 4.15 because her high school gives her extra points for her A grades in AP courses (though not for her As in her gifted student courses or her college courses at Michigan State University).

I've spent a lot of time on GPA and standardized testing because these factors greatly influence an applicant's chance of gaining admission to the college or university of their choice. They are the basic gatekeeper metrics that an admission official will employ in deciding if an applicant is feasible or not. They won't guarantee admission to college but if an applicant's GPA and test scores are not up to par with the profile of the admitted student body, they will probably predict the receipt of the thin letter in late March or early April that says *Thanks but No Thanks* to your college application.

The School Visit

Before visiting a school, sign up for an information session, a campus tour, and if possible an on-campus interview. As soon as you know your travel dates, sign up online for your desired date and time of day. Alternatively, call the admissions office and inquire about the availability of information sessions, campus tours and interviews on the day you want to visit the campus. Appendix D will help you keep track of your campus visit and interviews with your child.

When you and your child visit a school, it will provide an information session with an admissions official and sometimes a student or two who will go into detail about the school's student life. The information session typically will cover the school's academic credentials and requirements, what distinguishes it from other schools, and what the school is looking for in prospective students. The session will review the school's admissions process, its financial aid process, and the life of a student on campus. These information sessions are so similar that I eventually came to think that I could give a presentation just as well as the admissions officer of whatever school we were visiting.

Your school visit should also include a tour of the campus with a student who works in the admissions office. The tour will focus principally on the social aspect of the campus although it is open to questions about academics. The tour guide's job is to convey the message that residential halls are dynamic living environments, the food plan is not abysmal, and there are ample extracurricular activities to balance out a student's academics.

In the rare event that you are not able to sign up for a campus tour or an information session, you might want to take the initiative and just show up and create your own tour.

When my daughter and I went to Smith College we had an hour to kill before the official tour. We walked around the campus and found a door open to the performing arts center. We went inside where we met a student working in the theater. We spent a half hour probing her for info about their theater department and got a complete tour of the facility. When we visited Carnegie Mellon, the admissions counselor who met with us arranged for my daughter to join the theater conservatory tour even though we hadn't reserved a space on the tour before we arrived. But even without the help of the counselor, if we had shown up when the tour started, I doubt that anyone would have kicked us out.

I honestly can't imagine a school sending you away if you show up on a day it is offering info sessions and campus tours. The info sessions are usually in large rooms including auditoria and lecture halls. The tours are offered by students who would love to have someone interested in what they are saying.

You probably won't get an on-campus interview if you show up unannounced. Although, Smith had no record of me reserving an interview for my daughter; when I told them I had reserved one online, they worked their schedules around to give her one.

Admissions folks are accommodating. It's in their nature. They are the inviting face of a school, not gargoyles at the gate. At least not until they have to decide who gets admitted and who doesn't.

Information about a school may also be available through admissions counselors who meet with students in high schools and major urban areas. During the fall and again in the spring, collegiate admissions counselors travel throughout the country attempting to recruit students for their schools.

If a college or university has an admissions counselor coming to your child's school or to a city near you, I recommend she take advantage of the opportunity to make a connection as long as it is a school she has an interest in. Your child should introduce herself to the admissions counselor. She should get a business card and give the counselor one of her own, if she has one. Your child should follow up with a thank you note and express an interest in the school if the presentation tweaks her interest. This counselor is likely going to be one of the first readers of your child's application. She or he will be a more effective advocate for your child's application with the admissions committee if she or he knows something about your child and can speak intelligently to why your child should be admitted.

When you visit a college campus try to schedule a meeting with a faculty member in the academic area that interests your child. Generally, you have a better chance of setting up such a meeting if you visit the college or university during the school year.

Also schedule an on-campus interview, if possible. Not all colleges and universities offer interviews when you visit their campus. The University of Michigan doesn't. Harvard, Northwestern, and MIT didn't when we visited. Check to see on a school's website what its interview policy is.

If the school offers interviews during a campus visit, it will typically have a web form to use to sign up. Keep in mind these interview slots fill up quickly especially around key dates like your high school's spring break. Keep checking to see when the opportunity to schedule an interview goes live to make certain not to miss out on a chance to sign up.

Most of the interviews my daughter had when we visited colleges last summer were with students and one or two were with professional admissions counselors. Her interviews at Swarthmore, Smith,

Yale, Kenyon and Oberlin were with students who worked in the admissions office.

At the conclusion of the on-campus interview, parents are usually included in order to answer any questions they may have. Here is your chance to be your child's champion. You know your child's strengths that you want colleges to take note of. You should ask questions that showcase these strengths. For instance, my daughter was looking for a school with a strong theater department. I opened up with questions about the school's theater program and facilities and wove into the subsequent conversation what my daughter had accomplished in theater to date. I did the same with her work as a computer science education advocate and founder of the club Students for Females in STEM.

It is sometimes difficult for a child to blow their own horn when interviewing with an admissions office representative. It is extremely natural for a parent to brag on their child. No one will hold it against a parent and may be surprised if they don't.

Keep in mind that questions about Advance Placement policy are best addressed to the school's registrar and specific questions about a family's potential for financial aid should be addressed to the school's Financial Aid Office. We stopped by both of these offices at several schools we visited. The representatives of these offices are quite accommodating and more knowledgeable than a student tour guide or interviewer or even a staff member in the admissions office.

Some colleges and universities will offer a Junior Day during the year when parents and their children can attend for a day. The day may include an information session, a campus tour, a chance to eat in a residential hall or school cafeteria, access to admissions officials and financial aid officials, a chance for parents to ask questions in a session while their children attend classes. Schools usually don't offer interviews. I took my daughter to one of these Junior Days at Denison University where I went to school. Denison is a test optional school and one of the schools listed on the website, *Colleges that Change Lives*.

In addition to special events like Junior Days, some colleges may band together to offer a multi-campus tour where you visit schools that share an athletic league, common geography, or cross-school course registration. These events are usually published well in advance on a school's website. When we went to Kenyon, they were participating in a three-day promotion billed as an Ohio College Tour that included Kenyon, Oberlin, Denison, and Ohio Wesleyan. You can check the web for similar associations or collegiate affiliations that schedule shared admissions events.

Visiting colleges has become a big business. A company in Florida, grandcollegetours.com, promotes a three-day commercial tour of nine colleges and universities at a cost of $699 per student. College-visits.com offers seven-day tours in California, the Northeast, and the Southeast at a cost ranging from $1,895 in the Southeast to $2,185 in the Northeast. Education Unlimited offers seven-day tours of east coast colleges ($2,570) and California colleges ($2,675).

Whatever approach parents take, private self-guided tour or commercial tour, there is a cost involved in visiting schools. Use of vacation time, transportation costs including airfare, car rentals, tolls and parking wherever you go, lodging and meals can add up. I think I spent about $2,000 touring schools in the East Coast and the Midwest over a two-week period in June.

My daughter and I visited 11 colleges and universities in ten days. When were weren't on campus, we were in a car, usually fighting rush hour traffic, to get to our motel and the next day's college visit.

One word of caution: make sure you have a confirmed reservation. I had reserved a quaint bed and breakfast in downtown Philadelphia using a booking website, only to find the owner had double booked the reservation and had no place for my daughter and me to sleep. We had to scramble and find a motel near the airport which put us an additional half hour from the college we were to attend the next day and increased the lodging cost by a third.

Even with these setbacks, I worry that if parents and their children take a commercial tour approach, they lose some flexibility over their schedule. For example, we attended an information session and college tour of Harvard in the morning and the same at MIT in the afternoon. By the time we were done with half of the afternoon tour at MIT, both my daughter and I had had enough of fresh-faced college sophomores telling us how great their school was. We bugged out of the rest of the tour, took the subway back to our car and high tailed it out of the Boston metro area ahead of rush hour on our way to New Haven, which was our next stop.

If you have a lot of geography to cover to look at the various universities and colleges that your child wants to explore, just make certain to be willing to go with the crowd on a commercial tour when a school or its presentation doesn't really concern you. For example, a commercial tour might include schools you are not interested in visiting. The businesses referenced above all visit Ivy League and other top colleges. If your child is not likely to be accepted at Harvard or Johns Hopkins, why should you waste your time visiting their campuses?

Finally, visiting a college or university may be important to show a school your child is interested in it. Some but not all schools place an emphasis on Demonstrated Interest. Schools like Denison say they value an applicant's interest when reviewing their application. Therefore, the more connection your child has with a school and its personnel, the more she demonstrates interest in attending the school.

US News and World Report national rankings include the yield rate of an admitted applicant pool. The higher the yield of admitted students, the more prestigious the school is assumed to be. In other words, schools are looking for students who will enroll if they are accepted. Demonstrated Interest is one way they measure an applicant's likelihood to enroll.

This desire for a high yield from an admitted class may explain why students are accepted at reach schools and rejected by safety or match schools. If a school thinks an applicant is using them as a fall back with no demonstration of interest in their written application materials or a history of engagement with the school, then the school may reject them in lieu of accepting less credentialed students with a greater enthusiasm for attending.

Narrowing the List

A review of written materials and websites promoting colleges and universities followed by on-campus visits should give you and your child a working idea of what schools she wants to attend. Now it is time to narrow this vague impression to a concrete list of schools that fall into three categories:

- Safety Schools where a student's academic credentials exceed the school's range for the average freshman;
- Match Schools where an applicant's grades, standardized test scores and class rank match up with the average of the school's student body metrics;

- Dream or Reach Schools where a student's metrics fall below the average of the school's student body or where the admission rate is so low, they are a reach for even the most qualified student.

It is advisable to select at least two safety schools, two to three schools where an applicant matches up with the student body stats, and two to three reach schools.

My daughter applied as a potential computer science major to Purdue's School of Engineering (60% rate of admission), University of Illinois' School of Engineering, and Michigan State University's School of Engineering (86% rate of admission) as her safety schools. She wasn't aware, nor was I, that the Department of Computer Science in Illinois's School of Engineering had an 8% admit rate.

Her one match school consisted of just the University of Michigan, (42.5% admission rate for in-state applicants). Contrary to what I said above, she applied mostly to reach schools. Her reach schools were

- Harvard (5.4% admission rate),
- Yale (6.3% admission rate),
- Princeton (6.5% admission rate),
- MIT (7.9% admission rate),
- Duke (11% admission rate),
- Northwestern (10.7% admission rate), and the
- School of Computer Science at Carnegie Mellon (5% admission rate).

The thing to note about the reach schools listed above is that they are reach schools for all applicants. Gaining admission to any of these has been described as a lottery since more than half of the applicants are qualified to do the work if admitted. At the Yale information session, we were told 85% of their applicants were qualified for admission.

Why choose more than one school in each category? Because the admissions process can appear illogical to even the most *go with the flow* parent or student. My daughter was invited to apply to the Honors College at the University of Michigan. The U of M admissions office deferred her application to their Honors College and Purdue notified her that she was denied admission to its Honors College even though she never applied. It is almost impossible to understand how a student who has been accepted into Yale and was a finalist for a full ride scholarship at Duke doesn't qualify for Honors at the University of Michigan or Purdue. Trying to apply a rational approach to college admission is a task destined to failure.

Application Costs

Cost can also be a factor to consider when compiling a list of schools to which your children will apply. Application fees range from $60 to $90. With my daughter applying to 11 schools, we had to pay about $800 on application fees; and another $300 or so to send ACT and SAT scores to the schools, about $100 to send SAT Subject Test scores, and about $175 to send AP scores.

If a student knows what schools he or she wants to apply to, she can reduce the cost of sending them scores. Both the SAT and the ACT allow a test taker to select up to four schools to send test results for free when signing up for a test. However, if you opt to send scores to schools when you sign up to take a standardize test, the schools will see scores that you may not want them to see. This is especially true for schools that give applicants the choice over what test scores to submit with their applications. For schools that require the submission of scores for all tests taken, there is no reason not to take advantage of sending the scores to these schools when you sign up for the test.

The International Student

The American collegiate and university system has become the darling of the world. As middle classes emerge in countries like China, the demand from outside the US for a college education in the US has exploded. There were about 427,000 international students at US colleges and universities in 2015-2016. This represents a 79% increase over the number of students enrolled in 2005-2006.

Much of this demand focuses on the top colleges and universities. From 2000 to 2013, international student enrollment at state flagship universities increased 29% while over the same period enrollment increased 42% at top 25 research universities and 41% at top 25 liberal arts colleges.

International students are valued applicants because they usually pay full fare to attend a college or university in the US. Scholarship funds are not as generous for students outside the US. In spite of their financial reward to the schools that admit them, the admission rates for international students are usually lower than for US students. For instance, in 2012 the overall admit rate for applicants to MIT was 8.9%, while the admission rate for international students was 3%. According to Michelle Hernandez, most schools in the US limit their international student population to 10% of the overall class.

In other words, international applicants have a more rigorous road to travel to attend a US college or university. But many are not deterred. When my daughter and I attended the MIT information session, there were families from Japan, France and Columbia in the room.

The process an international student must go through to secure admission to an American school is the subject of a book in and of itself. This book is focused on the US student and her parents who are trying to make sense of the process and hopefully reach a happy ending where the student matches up with her preferred college or university.

The Community College Option

When my daughter interviewed at Smith College, the student conducting the interview suggested that she should have saved money on her education by going to a community college for the first two years of college and transferring into Smith as a junior. This option sounds appealing, especially if one's Expected Family Contribution is high. However, it is not as easy to do for private colleges with low attrition rates.

If a student is interested in transferring into a four-year college from a two-year community college program, she should first check the four-year college's admission rate for transfer students. Transition from community college to a four-year college is more likely to succeed if the four-year college is a public university in the state where the community college is located. For example, Yale has a 2-3% transfer admission rate. The University of Michigan-Ann Arbor, on the other hand, has a transfer admission rate of 40%.

The College Board which administers the SAT has a section of its website devoted to students who plan on attending a community college and transferring after two years to a four-year college or university. In preparing to transfer, the basic questions that the transferee needs to answer are:

- Is there a formal transfer agreement between a transferee's community college and the four-year school she wants to attend?
- Will all of a transferee's community college credits transfer?
- If not, which college credits will transfer?
- What grades are needed for a community college credit to transfer?
- What is the minimum GPA a transferee needs to transfer?

For high school students who are trying to save money on their four years in college, who don't know what they want to study, or who don't know where they want to study, a community college two-year degree may be worth pursuing. Community colleges typically are closer to home and may allow students to live at home and combine work and study while they prepare for transfer to a larger public university or private college further from home.

For students who didn't perform well in high school, the two-year community college option may work to their advantage. We all mature at different stages and to differing degrees. I didn't really find my footing in academia until my junior year in college. Before that I was teetering on the verge of failure. If a student can't get into the college or university they want to attend with their academic record in high school, community college gives them a second chance to show what they are capable of.

In sum, there are a variety of reasons why a student would want to wait before attending a four-year college. Exploring the community college option may make more sense than taking a gap year off from school. If a high school student does take this path, she will want to make certain that the four-year college she wants to attend later will likely have room for her.

Can I Get into a Top School?

In today's college marketplace, the demand for a top college or university has infected the passions of both students and their parents. Yale had 32,900 applications in 2016. Columbia had an all time high of 37,389. Stanford received 44,073 applications. And Cornell had more than 47,000.

Punching a winning ticket in the elite college admissions lottery requires mastering a "holistic admissions" process. If one is looking to apply to an elite school like Harvard with an admit rate of 6%, it would be wise to understand how the Ivy League and other top schools approach the admissions process.

First they will look at an applicant's qualification metrics. These include the high school GPA in a schedule of college preparatory courses that include honors, AP and college dual-enrolled classes. An applicant should have a weighted GPA above 4 and as close to an un-weighted 4.0 as she can get. Next, they will look at standardized test results in either the SAT or ACT. Again, the higher the score the better. Most of the admitted students in an Ivy League School are going to come from the 98th percentile of test takers or higher. That means a score of 32 on the ACT or 1470 on the SAT both of which put the applicant at or near the 25th percentile of admitted students' scores at most Ivy Leagues. Finally, an applicant will take at least two SAT Subject Tests. Shoot for perfect scores. For instance, in the Math 2 subject test, 12% of the test takers scored a perfect score of 800 in 2016.

The Ivy League schools use what is called an **Academic Index** (AI) to rank all applicants. Ostensibly the AI was developed to determine whether an athlete was capable of meeting the academic challenge of the Ivy League. But in order to rank the athlete who applies, the admissions office has to rank all applicants using the same metrics. For a detailed explanation of how the **Academic Index** works, I refer you to the book *A is for Admissions: The Insider's Guide to Getting into the Ivy League and Other Top Colleges* by Michele Hernandez, EdD.

The **Academic Index** uses a basic formula that treats equally

- GPA coupled with Class Rank,
- Standardized Test Scores, and
- SAT Subject Test Scores.

Each area is worth a maximum of 80 points and a perfect index score is 240. A valedictorian with an un-weighted 4.0 in a college prep course load would receive 80 points. If she also had a perfect score on her SAT or ACT composite test, she would get another 80 points. And if she had an 800 on each of two SAT Subject Tests she would get a final 80 points for a perfect score of 240. There are very few perfect applicants.

The minimum score an athlete attending an Ivy League has to have is 172. The average AI for all admitted freshman at Harvard, Princeton and Yale is 221. There are websites where one can calculate one's **Academic Index**. Note that each school which employs an **Academic Index** has its own approach to tweaking an applicant's GPA and class rank so one can never get an exact reading from web-based AI calculators.

Generally, the Ivy League School will group students' AI scores. Some schools use four groupings. Dartmouth uses nine. Admissions officials then consider the admissibility of applicants usually from the top three or four groupings out of nine or the top two out of four. So using the AI formula, applicants to an Ivy League or other top college can get a fairly good idea of where they stand. If they are at the bottom of the pile, their chance of admission is fairly slim. If on the other hand they are an 8 or a 9 (225 and above) or say a 1 and 2 out of 5 at Princeton, they have a good shot at being admitted, assuming the rest of their application measures up.

I found the **Academic Index** useful in trying to calculate my daughter's chances for admission to the very rigorous schools she applied to including Harvard, Princeton, Yale and MIT. She is not at the top of the scale (probably a 7 out of 9), but she isn't at the bottom either. It gave us some assurance that her applications weren't just a waste of time and money. As it was, Yale accepted her as an early admission applicant. Additionally, she was a finalist for a full ride Robertson Scholarship at Duke which is ranked among the top ten in the country by most ranking systems. She was waitlisted at Harvard and MIT and rejected by Princeton, so the AI is not a guaranteed predictor of admission.

If an applicant's **Academic Index** places her in the ballpark, then she should get a closer look.

The elite colleges and universities will next consider the depth of an applicant's commitment to something other than academics. Did she start a non-profit, develop a research project that merited publication, win a state or national award as an athlete, artist, or scientist? Does she have a passion for excellence or is she someone who has spread herself thin in order to try to impress the admissions officials with her extracurriculars? The latter are considered resume builders and don't fare well when the admissions committee meets to review applications.

Does the applicant have a love of learning that her teachers will confirm when they write her letters of recommendation? Is the applicant one of the most exceptional students they have taught and will they commit this to print?

Is the applicant a leader who has given back in an effort to help others less fortunate than she? How pervasive is her commitment? For example, does the applicant volunteer at a local hospital just so she can say she has volunteered somewhere or does she really want to contribute to her community's health and well being? Will someone back up her commitment with a positive supplemental recommendation?

Is she a legacy or a first generation college student? These factors could help an application although in themselves they are not determinative.

Then there is the narrative the applicant creates for herself in her own words. Your child's essay will show the admissions office what she values the most about herself. It should be authentic and interesting. An applicant wants the person reading her essay and written responses to supplemental questions to finish with the impression that she is someone the reader wants to know more about, preferably as an admitted student.

It goes without saying that all written responses including the essay should be free of typos, grammatical errors and misspellings. Your child should seek out a teacher in her high school who can proofread her essay and other written responses for errors. Generally, this will be an English teacher who has read many student essays over several years and knows your child well enough to suggest edits for clarity's sake.

For many top schools, the interview takes place after the school receives an application for admission. In this case, your child should make certain that when interviewing with an alumnus or admissions office representative, her oral narrative is consistent with her written one. Even though your child will most likely be nervous when interviewing, she shouldn't forget to be as likable as she knows how to be. Elite schools are looking for highly competent students who will work in a team atmosphere to build up their fellow students as well as themselves. Keep in mind that top colleges are putting together a distinctive entering class where students will have an opportunity to learn from each other as well as from their professors. The interview can help demonstrate that your child is just such a student.

A factor some top schools consider is demonstrated interest. One can use the **Common Data Set** to determine whether a school values demonstrated interest or not.

Elite schools that value an applicant's interest take note of whether she visited the school or met with an admissions counselor when he toured the applicant's region. Applicants also demonstrate interest by applying early.

There appears to be an advantage to applying early. Early decision and early action applications tend to have a higher admission rate. For example, in 2016, 8.4% of MIT's 7,767 early action applicants were admitted. Out of MIT's 16,029 regular decision applicants, only 5.1% were admitted.

In the final analysis, an applicant to a top school is tasked with showing the school what makes her stand out from the thousands of applicants who have the leadership and leverage required of admitted students. And you and your child shouldn't be disappointed if after doing all of this, she ends up on the short end of the stick. At the end of the day, an elite school like Stanford, Harvard or MIT is a reach school for nearly every applicant.

Am I Good Enough?

I said I wasn't going to address the issue of anxiety in the college admissions process, and I don't intend to change my position with one exception. Writing as a parent, I am deeply troubled by the emotional turmoil our children are undergoing in the college admissions gauntlet. Even the most accomplished high school student today seems filled with anxiety and self-doubt during her transition from home to college. Websites like collegeconfidential.com and Quora.com are replete with postings from high-schoolers asking whether they are qualified for this college or that college with only a 3.9 GPA and 1500 SAT Scores and a list of extracurriculars that include president of the chess club, captain of the football team, and volunteer at the local homeless shelter. Even the C student is asking what he must do to become a B student and get into a better college.

College education in these young adults' minds has become a desired commodity that comes with a price tag of spectacular accomplishments. Each year the college admission performance standards seem to grow in magnitude with ever increasingly elevated stress placed on the lives of 17 and 18-year-old children. How do we, parents, stop this spiral of suffering our children are undergoing?

College should be about personal development and social acclimation. Our children should be looking at a college and asking if it will fit their need for personal growth. As parents, we need to help our children realize that college is about them and their unfolding as human beings. Their college experience will resolve itself more in terms of what they bring to the school they attend than in terms of what external value the school has to impart.

We should be helping our children see that college is a launching pad into the world of work with a set of mental skills and insights that are beyond the scope of high school. We should be helping our children answer the question "How can I prepare for making a contribution to society and not go into deep debt doing it?" Instead, they seem to be worrying about how they can get into a name brand college that will stamp them as winners.

We are all losers in this emotional pressure cooker. You may take me to task for this position since my daughter was one of the fortunate ones who won the Ivy League Lottery. But I look at her admission to Yale with mixed emotions.

My ego is filled with pride but at what cost to my daughter? The rational parent in me asks if attending a school with her continuing expectation to perform at the highest level will serve my daughter's sanity and well-being. I know my daughter. She will want to excel in everything she does in college just as she has done in Montessori, middle school and high school. This desire is driven by an inner voice that has always challenged her as well as by a desire to not disappoint her peers, her teachers, and her parents. Occasionally, this pressure to not disappoint becomes too much for her and she is filled with pain and sadness. She feels like she has failed to measure up. Only love and reassurance can rescue her from this demon of self-doubt.

As we leave the college search and begin the college application process, we parents need to be mindful this step is fraught with risk for our children's mental health. They are going to put their sense of worth in the hands of strangers whose connection with them is always imperfect and mediated by metrics and narratives. They are going to ask these strangers to grant them admission, warts and all, into desired dorm rooms and classrooms for which they are the guardians at the gate. Our children are turning over control of their future to others who will pass judgment on them. Nothing about this next step in the process from home to college is easy or fun. Be gentle and understanding and above all, be the key adult who will champion their worth and their cause.

The College Application Process

The Common Application

In the olden days, colleges and universities had their own applications. Prospective students had to complete each school's individual application with pen and paper or a typewriter which tended to discourage one from submitting too many applications. They each had their own essay question and oftentimes supplemental questions. Teachers had to write letters of recommendation multiple times and the submission of standard documents like transcripts had to be monitored with vigilance so no school was left out.

Today, most top colleges and universities use the online Common Application. But there are also other applications, notably the Universal College Application or the more recent Coalition Application that schools are beginning to accept as well. These applications can be filled out online over more than one sitting.

The idea behind these applications is to simplify the application process. Teacher, guidance counselor and supplemental recommendations can be entered once and shared among all of the schools to which a student applies. Basic student information is entered once and made available to the schools the student elects to share it with. The common application includes a list of standard essays questions. A student selects one from the list and submits one written essay that all schools will see. Schools that want to include additional questions for their applicants can add them to the common application and the student doesn't have to go to another online application form to answer them.

When the student is done with the common application, she doesn't have to complete anything else in order to apply other than

- contact Parchment.com to arrange to send her official high school transcript to the schools she applies to,
- contact the College Board to send SAT and SAT Subject Tests, and
- contact ACT to send their ACT scores to their chosen colleges and universities.

She only needs to contact the College Board and/or ACT if she didn't arrange to send her scores to schools when she signed up for the tests.

The advantage of using the Coalition Application is that your child can begin as early as ninth grade to create a student profile, including the creation of a portfolio of documents that showcase her extracurricular activities and academic successes. The Coalition Application was designed in part to encourage under-represented and economically disadvantaged students to apply to college. The Coalition Application is intended to be a platform that students can use to explore the college selection process early on in their high school career as well as submit college applications when they have decided what schools they are interested in attending. It is still too early to know if the Coalition Application will supplant the more widely used Common Application.

Keep in mind that some colleges and universities such as MIT have their own online application which requires additional effort and responses to different questions than are found on the Common Application.

Keep Current

It is important to pay attention to timelines and deadlines associated with the application process. While several months to complete an online common application you can submit to all your schools in one day may seem like a lifetime; in truth it is an eye blink.

The class of 2021 was able to begin using the common application in August of 2016. However, the high school guidance counselor and teachers who needed to be asked to submit recommendations were on vacation and not due back in school until September. So practically speaking a high school senior in 2016 could not complete a college application until school started.

If your child is considering an early application, she only has until the beginning of November to complete it. Early Action and Early Decision deadlines are typically November 1 or November 15. Some schools do not accept early applications. Instead, all of their applications are due November 1.

Rolling admission schools have no deadline. They make admission decisions on a first come first served basis starting in August.

Early Action is used when you think you know what school you want to attend, but aren't certain. Early Decision involves a binding commitment to accept a school's decision to admit you, even if you don't know what its financial package will look like.

You have until May 1st to tell a school that has accepted you via Early Action that you will attend. Acceptance through Early Decision, on the other hand, nullifies all of your other applications and binds you to the school that has admitted you through Early Decision. The advantage of applying early is that your chances of being admitted improve if you are a qualified applicant. My daughter applied Early Action to Yale and was admitted. Something like 15% of the Early Action applicants were admitted to Yale last year compared to only 3% of the Regular Decision applicants for an overall admission rate of 6%.

Private colleges and universities that offer Early Action generally restrict how many private schools you can apply to early. Yale only allows an applicant to submit an Early Action to them if she is also applying Early Action to a public university or to a school with a rolling admissions policy.

Some schools like Michigan State University and Purdue University use a rolling admissions process which means that you usually get an answer to your application within two to four weeks after you apply. In the case of schools with a rolling admission policy, it is best to submit an application as early as possible. It is not uncommon for qualified applicants, who wait to apply to schools with rolling admission, to receive the "I'm sorry to inform you" letter.

You should check the website of the schools you are looking at to see what their application deadlines and policies are regarding early application.

Financial aid (FAFSA) applications can be submitted starting on October 1. The earlier the application is submitted, the greater the chance an applicant who is eligible will secure funding. If you are looking for additional scholarships to complement financial aid from a college or university, you need to keep in mind that scholarship deadlines are all over the place. It pays to buy a book with a comprehensive list of scholarships which will detail

- amount of aid,
- eligibility criteria,
- need-based status,
- application format, and
- deadline for submission.

Once you have identified a number of scholarships that your child may be eligible for, you will want to make a chart or calendar to keep track of when their applications are due (Appendix I).

For most colleges the deadline for Regular Decision applications is January 1 through February 1. If colleges are having a difficult time securing a significant number of applicants, they may open applications beyond their normal deadline but usually one should expect to submit a college application for Regular Decision between January 1 and February 1.

This deadline may seem like a lifetime until you take into consideration that the student who must complete the application with little assistance from anyone else is taking classes, engaging in several extracurricular activities, going to parties and movies with friends on the weekend, enjoying the freedom that comes with learning to drive, and in general being a teenager with a fluid sense of time.

No parent wants to spend their Christmas vacation standing over their child while she fills out a college application, writes a college essay, and tracks down a teacher or two on vacation to write a letter of recommendation by New Year's Eve. And yet if you don't pay attention to your child's progress in early fall, this nightmare scenario may become your reality.

Even with the most conscientious student, parents should expect pushback at some point in the application process. After all, the process of distilling your life into a series of written responses that can't be more than 250 words and an overall essay that is 500 to 650 words long is tediously difficult. And no matter how successful your child is, the thought that someone she doesn't know is sitting in judgment over her future is stressful. I had to push my daughter sometimes with more pressure than I wanted to impose in order to get her to complete her Regular Decision applications by the beginning of January. And she is not someone who usually pushes back when asked to do something for herself. So don't expect the process with its deadlines and pressures to go smoothly.

The Dreaded Essay Question

You can find websites, books, and even college application services that will assist students in writing the "winning" essay. Some more unscrupulous vendors will even offer to write an essay for applicants. This practice should be avoided at all costs. If a school discovers that an essay was purchased, it can and most probably will rescind its offer of admission.

The higher up the college food chain one goes, the more important becomes the way an applicant presents on paper. For The Ivies and other top schools, the applicant's college essay and answers to supplemental questions like *Why Do You Want to Attend (College Name Here)* are major stressors due to the importance these schools invest in the student's response.

The key, in my opinion, to writing a winning essay is to be authentic. Your child should write with her own voice, and try to create an impression that makes her seem so interesting that the reader, several admissions officials usually, will want to know more about her, preferably as an admitted student.

In my daughter's case, she shaped her narrative around her need to walk in two worlds — the theater and STEM. Her essay focused on her experience with theater and the difference it made in her life. The Common Application allows an applicant to submit additional information that is not covered by the essay prompts or the supplemental questions that some colleges and universities append to the Common Application. In the additional information section my daughter shaped a narrative around her advocacy efforts on behalf of females in Science Technology Engineering and Math (STEM).

The narrative your child tells of herself must be her own. You may be tempted to write your child's essay or arrange to have someone write it for her. This temptation must be avoided at all costs. Readers know when students are speaking and when adult or hired writers are. Don't rob your child of an opportunity to compete for a spot in the college of her choice because you don't trust her to speak her own truth.

This is not to say that adults don't have a role as editors and proof-readers. A well-written essay won't guarantee admission, but a mis-spelled essay with faulty grammar is a sure way to guarantee rejection or at best a wait-list admission at schools that place a high value on the essay.

Extracurricular Activities

Schools are looking for several qualities in the extracurricular activities of the students they admit which the written responses on the common application and the college interview should reflect:

- A love of learning;
- A passion for excellence;
- Leadership potential combined with a collegial attitude toward one's peers; and a
- Commitment to community engagement with a concern for those less fortunate.

Together these qualities make a spike that distinguishes an applicant from the majority of students who use their high school years building a resume with a large number of extracurricular activities they think schools will want to see.

I've read countless articles that say top schools are not looking for well-rounded students who are jacks-of-all-trades and masters of none. Instead they want well-rounded student bodies which are composed of students with highly developed skill sets and significant accomplishments that make them stand head and shoulders above their peers.

What works for a top school applicant should work for an applicant to a public university or liberal arts college. At the very least, if your child's extracurricular activities are representative of what she loves doing, she will come across more authentically in her application than a resume builder who lists ten things they do but spends less than an hour a week doing any one of them.

The Letter of Recommendation

These can make or break a borderline application. An applicant should consider very carefully whom she wants to write a letter of recommendation for her. Your child should first establish that her recommender believes she is qualified for the school of her choice before asking the person to submit a letter of recommendation on her behalf.

After all, your child is looking for an advocate who will be in her corner when it comes to persuading a college or university to admit her. You want someone who will identify how your child stands out among her peers. You also want someone so invested in your child's future that he will go the extra mile to connect with the admissions department by email or phone if necessary to promote her application.

Schools typically want teachers who are working with students during their junior year. They are looking for people who have the most immediate knowledge of a student's work habits and can confirm her extracurricular activities.

Your child should seek out teachers who think highly of her and know her work both inside and outside the classroom. This assumes she has made an effort to get to know her teachers and engage in their classroom with some degree of enthusiasm.

If your child has created a resume, she should share it with the teacher. The teacher will have something meaningful to say about her that is consistent with what your child is saying about herself.

If your child's academic record is not stellar, then you may want to supplement the teacher recommendations with non-teachers who will support her. If your child is active in church, she should seek out someone at the church to recommend her. Likewise, if she volunteers for Big Brothers/Big Sisters or Habitat for Humanity, she should secure a supplemental recommendation from the person who supervises her or the director of the organization.

If you can find an alumnus or someone otherwise attached to the school your child wants to attend to submit a recommendation on her behalf, it may add value to the recommendation process. The recommender will be more invested in the admissions decision and may even be persuaded to go a step further and contact the admissions office by phone or email on your child's behalf in order to draw attention to your child's application.

Regardless of who ends up recommending your child, she should send a thank you note and keep her recommender updated on the progress of her application. If she is going to ask someone to take the time to write a recommendation, she should repay the effort with courtesy and a note of gratefulness.

One recommender you have no choice over is your child's guidance counselor. Again, making a connection with the guidance counselor early in the college search process may help influence what she will say about your child. Generally, though, this recommendation goes to the issue of where your child stands relative to other students in the school and other relevant information about the school such as its AP course policy.

In addition, if there are personal issues that have impacted your child's performance in high school, the guidance counselor may be able to explain them in a way that minimizes the negative consequences of these issues. For instance, if your child was sick for a prolonged period of time and unable to keep up with her course work, your guidance counselor's recommendation can reference this setback and its impact on your child's GPA.

The College Interview

If your child doesn't interview when she visits colleges, she may have an opportunity to interview with an alumnus in your hometown. These interviews typically last between 30 and 45 minutes. It is unclear how influential the interviewer's evaluation is. Certainly, a bad interview can help defeat an application but a good interview may have a negligible impact on the admissions office's final decision about your child's application.

Some schools never conduct interviews. Others don't make interviewers available unless one applies. My daughter had mixed results with her interviews. The local Princeton alumnus rushed through his interview with her and left her feeling like she wouldn't fit there. On the other hand, her MIT interview with an astrophysics professor at Michigan State ran for an hour and a half and increased my daughter's appreciation of the school. Even though the interviewer was impressed with her, the MIT admissions office still decided to waitlist her.

My daughter is a naturally gregarious and well-mannered young adult. She interviews well because she is confident in her ability to engage with her interviewer. Not all students will be as confident. Some will obsess over the clothes they wear or will try to rehearse their responses to common questions so they don't freeze like a deer in headlights.

The more your child wants to be admitted to the school interviewing her, the more she may fear failure in her efforts. It doesn't hurt to conduct trial interviews with her before she encounters the real thing. But the main thing to impress on her is that the interview is designed for her to learn more about the school she is interested in from someone who was a student there. At the same time, it gives the interviewer a chance to see if the interviewed student would fit into the school's culture.

For students who can't interview face-to-face on campus or with a local college alum, schools are turning to technology like Skype to conduct interviews. When my daughter interviewed with the Robertson Scholarship Committee to see if they would move her from a semi-finalist to a finalist, the interview was conducted over Skype.

When using technology, the interviewee must be conscious of things like strength of Internet connection. A weak connection may disrupt the interview and leave the interviewee looking at a blank screen. An interviewee must also be conscious of the background that will be displayed on the interviewer's screen. In my daughter's case, she had a Chagall print in the background that the committee asked if she had painted. How one presents oneself in the frame will say as much about an interviewee as the words that come out of her mouth.

The question of fit works two ways. I've always told my daughter that she has nothing to lose in the narrative she creates for her application or the interview she has with a school representative. It wouldn't do any good for her to be admitted to a school where she will be miserable for the next four years. The interview is as much a chance for her to decide if she will fit into a school as it is a way for a school to see if she will fit its mold. When approached this way, the interview really becomes a mutual assessment between a school and a student to see if they match up with one another.

The four years my daughter will spend in college are her years. They exist to help her complete her development into adulthood. If she doesn't fit where she finds herself at school, her development will be stunted and her time wasted. In the final analysis the college search process comes down to finding a place where one can be true to oneself, not secure a brand that will mark one's future.

Digital Footprints

In this digital age with students owning smartphones, tablets, and personal computers all linked to the Internet, a digital footprint exists for colleges and universities to seek out and review before making their final decision on whether to accept an applicant or not. High school students may not realize that what they post on their Facebook page or publish on Instagram could end up in their application file.

You need to respect the privacy of your child's digital persona, but at the same time, you need to caution your child about the consequences of what she posts and publishes online. Schools can and have rescinded offers of acceptance to students based on their digital footprint.

Inside the Admissions Office

Jacques Steinberg is the authority on what transpires in the admissions office where the decision on who gets admitted, waitlisted or denied is made. He authored the definitive text, *The Gatekeepers: Inside the Admissions Process of a Premiere College*, published in 2002. Steinberg followed up his book with a blog at the *New York Times* called **The Choice Blog** which was closed down in 2013 when he retired.

Steinberg equates the opacity of the college admissions application review with that of the Conclave electing a Pope. To be sure, waiting for the email or letter which contains the decision the admissions office has made is as fraught with anxiety as waiting for the color of the smoke in St Peter's square.

From time to time newspapers, television networks, and radio stations like NPR will run a story about how admissions professionals evaluate students. Generally, these news accounts are fairly superficial and stress the difficulty admissions officers have selecting a freshman class out of an abundance of qualified candidates who would bring value to their schools. You can also find blogs usually created by for-hire college readiness consultants who purport to know how the admissions decision-making process works.

Certain things do stand out in what has been disclosed of the application review process. The first is that an application doesn't start out with a committee review or final decision of the admissions director. A counselor in the admissions office will do a first read of an application from a qualified application and prepare a one-page written summary. This reading may take place in the counselor's office. But it is just as likely to be read in their car in between school visits while they wolf down lunch. Or it may be the last thing an admissions counselor reads before trying to go to sleep in a noisy hotel room with bed bugs biting their back. Applicants should assume that their applications will be the ones read in competition with a stone hard mattress filled with bed bugs and make every effort to create a compelling and interesting narrative.

When your child asks her English teacher to proof read her essay, she should make certain to get feedback on how interesting the essay is. Interest is a quality that results in reader engagement. Does the person reading the essay come away from it with a sense that he wants to know more about the writer? Is the person illuminated in the written text someone who fits with the mission and values of colleges and universities today? Will this person in the text add value to any freshman class they enter regardless of the college they choose to attend? In other words, does the written narrative in the application lead the fatigued, anxious and overwhelmed admissions counselor, who is assigned the initial reading of the application, to pass the application on with a summary that says accept?

Pay close attention to the supplemental questions, if a college asks them. These questions require more concise responses. The rubric to be interesting is especially important with these questions, especially the one that asks why you want to attend the school. An authentic response will get more attention than a generality about "changing the world." Authentic does not mean an open book. If an applicant values a school because it has an excellent athletic program and he wants to try to make the football team as a walk-on, then he should say so. Admissions officials are looking for students who will fit in and if offered admission to the school, accept the school's offer. The more a qualified applicant's narrative aligns with the culture and values of the school she applies to, the more confident the admissions officer will be in accepting the applicant.

Keep in mind that the harried admissions counselor reviewing applications has a quota of students who must be admitted each year. The faculty are relying on the admissions office to find students who want to learn what they have to teach. The administration has a budget that relies on a set number of student enrollments each year to remain in balance. The President and Board of Trustees are worried about keeping the school's ranking among similar colleges and universities. A school's yield, the percentage of admitted students who accept its offer of admission, is a key factor in a school's ranking.

An application usually but not always receives a second reading by another, more senior admissions counselor. The second reader may have a deeper understanding of the region from which the applicant comes and can make a more reflective decision on how an applicant stands in comparison to other applicants in their region.

The second reader will rank the application if the college uses a ranking system or issue her own decision on whether to admit, waitlist or deny the applicant admission. If the rating of the first and second reader are the same, the application may pass on to the admissions director for final review and decision. If there is a disagreement between the first and second reader, a third reader may be asked to read and rate the application before it advances to committee. Likewise, if an applicant is borderline, her application may move onto an admissions committee for review and recommendation.

In the committee, the applicant may have advocates who support her admission as well as detractors. The decision to admit will in that case come down to a vote after a vigorous discussion. To get a sense of what this discussion boils down to, think about Twitter which limits tweets to 144 characters. An applicant's labored and thoughtful application may be summed up in a few descriptive statements and then voted up or down.

In anticipation of this tendency of busy people overwhelmed by life-altering decisions to abbreviate the significance of an applicant's diligent effort, applicants should try to figure out how their application will be summed up before submitting the application. For example,

- good student who plays it safe inside the lines and resume builder with no passion;
- low-income minority whom football coach wants for team and who can keep up with studies;
- concert violinist with top academics who can fill spot in school symphony orchestra and doesn't need financial aid.

The admissions committee can only accept one of these applicants. In the scenario above, the decision comes down to the athlete and the violinist. If the school is looking to increase its number of under-represented minorities and fill out its football team, the athlete is likely to get the nod. On the other hand, if the school's finances are an issue, the concert violinist who can pay for her education without financial aid will get the acceptance letter. In either case, the safe student with nothing distinctive about him will be denied admission.

A Note to Helicopter Parents

No matter how tempted you are to intervene on your child's behalf with the admissions office, resist at all costs. I made the mistake of sending the University of Michigan's Director of Admissions an email when the school deferred my daughter's application for the University's Honors College (Appendix J). I spelled out all the reasons why they should reconsider their decision and admit her to the Honors College. My argument was based on facts, not emotion. Convinced that my argument would persuade the admissions office to reconsider their decision, their response told me that my words fell on deaf ears. If anything, I guaranteed that they wouldn't take her off their waitlist and admit her. I don't think my daughter was happy with me either.

But when you are accepted at Yale, what the University of Michigan thinks of your application for its Honors College is basically meaningless. I was more upset with the University of Michigan than was my daughter, who had no problem dismissing it from the list of schools she considered attending.

I had based my experience on that of my mother whose intervention got my brother admitted to the University of Michigan in 1968. He was a student at Phillips Exeter and the school failed to send his transcripts and recommendations to the University of Michigan before their application deadline. His application was rejected. My mother, who was a legacy at the U of M in a long line of U of M graduates, called the admissions office and convinced the Dean to admit my brother largely because he was rejected as a result of his prep school's error and not his own academic record.

My mother did what any parent would do for a child. She interjected herself into my brother's application process to correct what she saw as an injustice caused by his school. But his situation was not my daughter's. She had submitted a timely application with all the required items included and was not admitted. My intervention, well intended as it was, was likely one of hundreds if not thousands the admissions office receives during the course of reviewing applications for its undergraduate program and its Honors College.

Admissions officials have to develop a tough hide to do their job. Parents stepping up and raising an appeal on their child's behalf don't advance the interest of their child. We are easily dismissed with prejudice. The admissions office may be open to communication from your child; but deans of admissions are not going to listen to a parent in place of a young adult who wants to be treated as such in the application process.

No matter how much you are tempted to take your child's case to the office of the Dean, stop. Take a deep breath. Ask yourself what your goal is. If there is room for an appeal of an admissions decision you don't agree with, then help your child ask the admissions office to review her application and if possible reconsider its decision. By all means, provide guidance on what the appeal should address, but put down the helicopter and let your child take the lead. She will be happier and it may actually achieve the result you both want. If you take to the air with rotor blades blasting, you can be certain neither you nor your child will arrive at the place you want to get.

The Admitted Student's Decision

Hopefully, your child's college search concludes with multiple offers of admission. Now your child has one final big decision to make — where to enroll? Once an applicant is admitted to a school, phase two of the college search process kicks in with aggressive marketing campaigns aimed at influencing the admitted student's decision of where to attend college in the fall.

This decision process really doesn't start until the spring of one's senior year unless one applies Early Decision or Early Action and accepts the Early Action offer of admission. Early Decision applicants are bound to the school that accepted them early. The only decision facing them is how to pay for their college education.

Your child should have a list of schools that have accepted her, assuming she has triaged her applications. She will have to select one by May 1· and let them know of her intent to attend in the fall. And Dad or Mom writes the deposit check that holds her place in the school.

As a courtesy, your child should notify the remaining schools which admitted her that she will not be accepting their offer. If your child is offered a place on a waitlist and she accepts it, she would not notify the wait-listing school. However, if she is waiting for possible admission off the wait list, your child still needs to decide on another college or university by May 1· and let it know she accepts its offer of admission.

Coping with No

If your child has included several reach schools among her applications, she will most likely get a rejection letter or two. Before she can turn her attention to those schools that have accepted her, she will want to work through her feelings arising from rejection.

Even before she starts her college career at Yale, my daughter had to confront a significant disappointment when the Robertson Scholars Program passed her over. She had to face this rejection with grace and resignation. It is never easy to put yourself forward and have someone say you are not up to their standards. This is a painful message to hear.

For many high school students reaching beyond their immediate circumstance for acceptance into a top college or university or for recognition of academic or athletic achievement, this message of No reverberates and leaves them deeply wounded. How your child deals with No goes a long way to determining how fruitful her college years will be. If she internalizes it as a judgment of her personal worth or value, she will deepen the wound more than it deserves. All your child can really do is feel the pain, own it for what it is, and move beyond it with assurance that the path toward Yes that she is on is the one that she is meant to follow.

A certain degree of fatalism never hurts in this instance. After all, we are not changed intrinsically by someone else's judgment. If anyone is affected ultimately by such judgments, it is the judger, not the judged. The school that rejects your child's application or the program that passes her over for an award has lost its connection with her.

My daughter remains the center of her world and she will make of it what lives within her spirit and her will. No one can take this freedom from her but herself. I know my daughter's heart. I know what she is capable of. Any responsible parent knows these things. I also know that the universities that waitlisted her or rejected her and the collegiate award programs that passed her over have lost more than she will ever lose. I take great comfort in this knowledge because I know what she will bring to the schools that have seen her value as a potential student and have given her a chance to be a part of their community.

I also know that there is no virtue in trying to be a part of something that doesn't want you to be a part of itself. Nothing that has happened in the application process will diminish my daughter's talent and ability. As soon as she sees this as well, she will be able to move on and thrive where she plants herself.

Financial Aid Offers

The decision of which school to attend will also include a review of offers of financial aid which don't start showing up until February for early action admits or late March/early April for regular decision admits. Schools set aside special information sessions for parents of children accepted at their school. I received numerous emails in March from Purdue informing me of their online chat room where parents of admitted students could confer with representatives of the Financial Aid office on Purdue's offer of aid.

You shouldn't feel that you have to accept the first offer of aid. It is typically the start of a process that involves a negotiation and comparison of offers among schools. Colleges and universities are used to parents trying to renegotiate initial aid packages when students are clearly academic standouts and are being recruited by multiple schools.

It never hurts to have a one on one conversation with a Financial Aid Officer to see if there is any room for change in their offer. You should be prepared to cite explanations for why you think you are entitled to more money. Some reasons that might find a sympathetic ear are:

- changes in employment status and income since completing the FAFSA and CSS/Financial Profile,
- the need for early retirement based on illness or disability,
- health care bills which are not covered by insurance,
- the need to save for the education of children coming next to the college admission pipeline, or
- a better offer from a competing school.

The Honors College

Many public and private colleges and universities have an honors program or residential college for their top admits. Generally, admission is based on a student's college application compared to the overall profile of the in-coming class. At large public universities, like the University of Michigan, admission to its Honors College requires a separate application with a separate essay and review.

As admission to elite colleges and universities becomes increasingly more competitive and lottery-like, high school students are turning more and more to honors programs and residential honors colleges as a substitute. This means the number of admitted students applying for honors programs and colleges is rising. Admission rates at honors colleges in a public Ivy like the University of Michigan are on par with admission rates at an Ivy League school like Harvard or Yale.

If your child is considering an offer of acceptance from a large university, you would want to help her determine whether she will be accepted into a school's honors program for first year students. This factor alone can turn the impersonal, lecture hall heavy, teacher assistant taught first year experience into the equivalent of a small, liberal arts college experience at a fraction of the cost for in-state students.

The Admitted Student Visit

Colleges and universities set aside a day or a weekend, usually in April, for admitted students to visit their campuses. These are the final marketing events designed to persuade students to accept a college's offer of admission. Your child will spend time on campus sitting in on classes, attending social functions, eating school food, receiving special attention from notable faculty in her intended major, and hanging out with college students and other admitted high school students in a college dorm overnight. It may be the first time your child separates from you to attend college, if only on a trial basis.

It is important that your child does her best to determine whether she fits in with the school she is visiting. If at all possible, she should visit as many schools' admitted student days or weekends as possible during April. Her decision will determine how much she benefits from the next four years of her life and beyond, depending on the friends for life she makes in college.

Deciding on a school is often an intuitive decision. Certainly objective factors matter like the

- school's strength in the major your child wants to pursue;
- student's cost of attendance;
- availability of advanced standing credits;
- likelihood of graduation in four years;
- scope of activities aligned with student's passions, and
- school's academic rigor and resulting level of stress.

School's Support for Major Interest

If your child has a clear idea of where she wants to concentrate her study at college, then the admitted visit is a good time to visit the department where she will major and talk with the faculty about their program. If she can't attend an admitted student event, she can look for indications of a department's strengths in national rankings. She can also look at a school's distribution of bachelor degrees by subject area in the school's Common Data Set to see what major areas the students value and whether the top majors they pursue align with her interest.

Advanced Standing

You can contact the school registrar and confirm what advance placement credits your child is likely to receive upon entering school. The final tally will not be known until the child takes her last AP tests in May for the AP courses she takes as a senior. At the same time, you should determine whether your child's dual enrolled college credits will be counted toward her degree. In this way, your child can know what her options for courses are if she enrolls and how many semesters or quarters she will need to earn a baccalaureate degree.

Graduation in Four Years

This conversation with the school registrar matters. At many large public universities, it has become increasingly more difficult to graduate in four years. One reason is that demand for the classes a student needs to graduate exceeds the availability of these classes in any given term. As a result, undergraduates are not able to complete in four years all of the university's core curriculum courses. You should seek reassurance from the registrar that your child will not have a problem accessing the school's required courses in four years. Any additional time in school spent on securing a degree increases the cost of college for both parents and student.

Alignment of Activities

If your child didn't explore a school's extracurricular opportunities when she was searching for schools, she should take a closer look at what a school has to offer during an admitted student visit. Does the school have a range of theatrical performance opportunities for the child who loves the stage as my daughter does? Will your child be able to play the sport he loves if he doesn't try out or make the college team? Does your child love to sing in a choir or play an instrument in a band? Is she an aspiring novelist who needs to have fellow writers help her work on her first novel? These passions and others require structure and opportunity. During her admitted school visit, your child will want to seek out students who share her passion and try to learn how well supported they feel at the school.

Academic Rigor and Resulting Stress

As a parent whose child will be attending an elite university, I worry about the stress she will be under to maintain the level of performance she achieved in high school. She is a dedicated student who has never had a B for a final grade in her life. Once she arrives at Yale, she will be thrown in with other gifted and talented students who are not accustomed to a poor grade either.

She is making the transition from the proverbial big fish in a pond to small fish in an ocean. Any experience of failure will be doubly hard. It is important to know how schools help their students cope with the pressures to succeed and the disappointments associated with setbacks. For some students, the transition is too great and the experience of setback too painful to continue with their education.

To gauge this compression of rigor and stress, your child really needs to talk frankly and openly about it with students at the schools she is visiting.

Marketing for Yield

Colleges and universities measure the success of their college admissions process by the proportion of admitted students who enroll. This number represents the admissions department's yield. The higher the yield, the more prestigious the school is said to be, at least according to the *US News and World Reports* ranking methodology.

In order to increase its yield, colleges and universities engage in a variety of marketing efforts.

Today colleges reach out to admitted students and their families through a variety of virtual interfaces starting with a school's announcement of its admissions decisions. College admissions decisions now arrive first in an email followed by a snail mail package a few days later for those students who are admitted.

Colleges and universities create Facebook pages for their admitted students to connect with the school and one another. Almost as soon as she heard from Yale, my daughter joined its Facebook community and began to interact with other students from her state and across the country. The use of this virtual community is apparently designed to both inform and solidify an admitted student's interest in committing to the brick and mortar school. After all, if you begin to interact with a group of students like you, you are more likely to stay engaged with them if the experience is positive.

Yale has also been the most aggressive in its effort to recruit my daughter with

- a personalized letter from the admissions counselor who read her essay,
- an email extolling its theater programs,
- an unsolicited offer to enroll her in its freshman directed studies program,
- a personalized invitation to attend its Bull Dog Days, and
- a follow up mailing that included a booklet describing its engineering school along with a copy of its magazine.

Colleges and universities connect with admitted students through glossy marketing materials, gifts and personal contacts. Yale sent my daughter a tee shirt along with a banner. Northwestern had a female student from its School of Engineering call my daughter offering to answer any questions she might have of the school. Carnegie Mellon sent a tartan banner and an Official Fat Letter that included a:

- VIP invitation to visit the campus,
- map of the campus for visiting on upcoming admitted student days,
- overview of housing and dining services on campus,
- highlight of those experiences of student life that create the basic culture of the university,
- tourist's guide to Pittsburg, and
- collection of orientation publications for students ready to commit.

Purdue and Illinois sent multiple postcards and other mailings including, in the case of Illinois, a personalized letter from the Dean of the Department of Computer Science. Knowing of her interest in STEM, Michigan State University repeatedly invited my daughter to engage with its Women in STEM faculty group. The University of Michigan, consistent with its school first, students second attitude, reached out the least of any schools who accepted my daughter.

In addition to its financial aid chats, Purdue aggressively offered online chat sessions for parents to ask any questions they might have. Duke created a Facebook community for the parents of admitted students to begin to cement a parental connection with the University. It appears they are hoping this connection will motivate parents to influence their child's commitment decision.

The Parental Role

The colleges and universities who have admitted your child may want you to weigh in on her choice of school to attend. The most difficult thing for you to do in this moment of truth is letting your child make the final decision of where she wants to go. If you provide any type of guidance, try to help your child structure the parameters of this difficult decision.

For example, students deciding what school to attend need to know the financial consequences of their decision. Your child needs to know what you are prepared to do in making it possible to return home during the school year if she chooses to go to a school some distance from her parental home.

Or if you are not equipped to pay the full *Expected Family Contribution* of attending college, then you should let your child know how much debt she will have to assume for each school she is considering. Your child will also need to know if attending a certain school will necessitate getting a job to pay for part of the cost of attendance.

You may want to talk to the dean of the college or academic department your child wants to pursue. You should explore their pedagogical philosophy. Some engineering schools take the approach that incoming students need to be challenged to the point of breaking down so they can be reworked into the mold of the school.

Another question you may want to pursue is the school or department's approach to advising students. Will your child be expected to navigate the path to a degree pretty much on her own or will her academic advisor play an active role in guiding her through the policies and procedures that dictate her course of study?

You may want to inquire about the mentoring and tutoring services that are available to support your child's transition to a college curriculum. Another reason students are spending more than four years to acquire a bachelors degree is their failure to seek advice on what they need to do to graduate in four years or even less. During her admitted students' tour of the School of Computer Science at Carnegie-Mellon, the faculty emphasized access to tutoring, academic advising and personal counseling as some of the School's core responsibilities to its students.

You may want to help your child determine whether the school's facilities are up to par. Are the science and computer labs cutting edge? If your child is interested in performing arts, what is the condition of their rehearsal spaces and performing halls and theaters? If your child is interested in athletics, do the training facilities and playing fields support her desire to expand her skills and compete at the highest level of her ability?

Your child may be swept up in the enthusiasm that comes from being accepted at the end of the college admissions gauntlet and not look closer into whether the schools she is deciding among have all that she needs and wants for her education. It is the parents' responsibility to take a sober view of the opportunities offered by each school that has accepted their child and help her arrive at an objective assessment of each school's true value.

Make no mistake, this decision is not an easy one to make if your child has a breadth of schools to choose from. My daughter was deeply torn in her decision. She recognized the value of the three schools she visited on admitted students' days: Yale, Carnegie Mellon and Northwestern University.

Each school had both strengths and weaknesses. In the end, she chose Yale, largely because she realized that she would have a more diverse experience at Yale. Her mother and I shared her belief that Yale provided a stimulating culture that would go beyond what she has experienced in her life to date.

However, we did not make the decision for her. Instead we gave her reinforcement for the choice she was leaning toward. I firmly believe parents should not decide for their child what school to attend and then work at subverting any alternative choice she may be prepared to make.

Once your child has made a decision, she will be looking to you for support — both emotional and financial. If you disagree with her decision, try not to show your disappointment. You have been a guide in this process, not the owner of it. Your child's happiness and further growth as a person are the destinations all parents should be working toward. Both will be severely tested if you express any reservation with your child's final choice for college.

The Waiting List

Some applications may result in an offer to be waitlisted at a college or university. Qualified applicants are invited to accept their waitlisted status and wait until after May 1ˢᵗ to see if the school has an opening for them.

Is it a good idea to accept this limbo status? In part it depends on the student's desire to attend the school. It also depends on whether you, the parent, are prepared to forfeit your deposit at another school where your child accepted admission prior to May 1ˢᵗ.

You and your child should not view a waiting list as anything more than a narrow door through which very few qualified, waitlisted students will pass. In no way should your child forfeit all other options for attending college/university in the fall while waiting for the school that has waitlisted her to decide on admitting her.

You can go to the Common Data Set for the school that waitlists your child to see what proportion of students waitlisted are actually admitted. For example, in 2016 Princeton waitlisted 1,237 applicants. Of this number, 840 (72%) accepted a place on its waiting list. Of the 840 qualified applicants on the waiting list, Princeton admitted 18 (2%). The University of Michigan offered 14,960 qualified applicants a place on its waiting list in 2015. Of this number, 4,512 (30%) accepted a place on the waiting list. The University admitted 90 (2%) waitlisted students.

As you can see, the chance of moving from a school's waiting list to admitted student status is remote.

The Gap Year

Once an applicant has decided what school they want to attend and notified the school of their decision, one final option in the application process remains. Some students choose to take a year off from school before enrolling. This is known as a gap year. The school your child decides to attend agrees to keep her admission open while she does something else during this year.

If your child is interested in a gap year, then she needs to know if the school she wants to attend will allow for one.

Summary

I hope I have not overwhelmed you with information that you already know or with too much detail if you just wanted some general observations of the college admissions game. My basic premise is that colleges and universities, whether they are at the top of the rankings or not, are looking for students who:

- will thrive in their learning environment;
- have a passion for more than study whether it is video games or world peace;
- can manage the academic rigor of the school they attend without undue pressure or stress;
- will add value for both the school and their classmates;
- know what they want out of the school they attend; and
- will realize the potential that others see in them.

College is an incubator, not an end point. Students pass through on their way to full adulthood and social accountability. Colleges take their mission to prepare their students for this transition as seriously as they take their other important roles to build on humanity's collective knowledge and to generate prosperity for their communities and beyond. In the end, college is an inviting place that regrettably has to decline admission for too many qualified candidates. But with over 2,400 public and private four-year institutions enrolling nearly 11,000,000 students, a student intent on attending one will find her path to Yes and begin her journey toward a richer and more rewarding life than high school has to offer.

I've tried to cover all that I've read or experienced about the college search and application process. I recognize that your child's junior and senior years in high school may be a stressful time for both your child and for you as it was for our daughter and us, her parents. There are no shortcuts or magic bullets that make this process an easy one. As Sly of Sly and the Family Stone said long ago, "In order to get to it, you have to go through it."

If, after reading this book, you have questions feel free to email me at findingyourpathtoyes@gmail.com or look for me on Quora where I seem to be answering the same questions over and over again.

Appendix A: Student Resume

Student's Name

School, Grade, and Graduation Year:

Cumulative GPA:

Best ACT and SAT:

Five Words that Describe Me:

Career I Am Considering:

Passion:

Other Strong Interest:

Other Leadership Roles:

Volunteerism:

Summer Activities:

Awards:

Other Notable Projects:

Appendix B: School Profile Checklist

Appendix B: School Profile

School
Address
City / State / Zip
Website
Admissions Phone Number
Admissions Email Address
Nearest Metropolitan Area
Institution Type
Coeducational
Academic Calendar System
Entrance Difficulty
Overall Admission Rate
Early Action Offered
Early Decision Offered
Regular Admission Deadline

Academic and non-academic factors considered in admissions

	Very Important	Important	Considered	Not Considered
Academic				
Rigor of secondary school record				
Class rank				
Academic GPA				
Standardized test scores				
Application essay				
Recommendations				
Nonacademic				
Interview				
Extracurricular activities				
Talent/ability				
Character/personal qualities				
First generation				
Alumni/ae relation				
Geographical residence				
State residency				
Religious affiliation/commitment				
Race/ethnic status				
Volunteer work				
Work experience				
Level of applicant's interest				

SAT and ACT Policies

	Require	Recommend	Require for Some	Consider if submitted	Not Used
SAT or ACT					
ACT only					
SAT only					
SAT and SAT Subject Tests or ACT					
SAT Subject Tests only					

Act with Writing Component Required	
ACT with Writing Component Recommended	
ACT with or without Writing Component accepted	

	SAT Essay	ACT Essay
For admission		
For placement		
For advising		
In place of an application essay		
As a validity check on the application essay		
No college policy as of now		
Not using essay component		

	Required	Recommended	Minimum Score
Test of English as a Second Language Exam			
International English Language Testing System			

Source: Common Data Set Initiative

Appendix B: School Profile

Academics	
Full Time Faculty	
Student to Faculty Ratio)	

Class Size	% of Classes
2-9 Students	
10-19 sutdents	
20-29 students	
30-39 students	
40-49 students	
50-99 students	
Over 100 students	

Special Study Options	
Accelerated Program	
Cooperative education program	
Cross-registration	
Distance learning	
Double major	
Dual enrollment	
English as a Second Language	
Exchange student program (domestic)	
External degree program	
Honors program	
Independent study	
Internships	
Liberal arts/career combination	
Student-designed major	
Study abroad	
Teacher certification program	
Weekend college	
Other	

Core curriculum areas	
Arts/fine arts	
Computer literacy	
English (including composition)	
Foreign languages	
History	
Humanities	
Mathematics	
Philosophy	
Sciences (biological or physical)	
Social science	
Other	

Source: Common Data Set Initiative

Appendix B: School Profile

Enrollment and Persistence

Institutional Enrollment by race and ethnicity	Degree-seeking first-time first year	Degree seeking undergraduates (include firsti time, first year)	Total Undergraduates
Nonresident aliens			
Hispanic/Latino			
Black, African-American, non-Hispanic			
White, non-Hispanic			
American Indian or Alaska Native, non-Hispanic			
Asian, non-Hispanic			
Native Hawaiian or other Pacific Islander, non-Hispanic			
Two or more races, non-Hispanic			
Race and/or ethnicity not known			

Institutional Enrollment	Male	Female	Total
Undergraduate Students			
Graduate Students			

	Percentage	Countries
International Students		

Four year graduation rate	

Six year graduation rate	

Source: Common Data Set Initiative

Appendix B: School Profile

Housing
Types of Housing

Coed Dorms	
Men's Dorms	
Women's Dorms	
Apartments for married couples	
Apartments for single students	
Special housing for disabled students	
Special housing for international students	
Fraternity/sorority housing	
Cooperative housing	
Theme housing	
Wellness housing	
Other housing options	

Freshmen housing guaranteed	

Security

24-hour emergency phone/alarm devices	
24-hour security patrols	
Late night transport/escort services	
Electronically operated housing entrances	
Other	

Personal Support Services	Offered
Health Service	
Personal Counseling	
Child Care	

Sports and Recreation

Athletic Conference	
Women's Club Sports	
Men's Club Sports	
Intramural Sports	

Source: Common Data Set Initiative

Appendix B: School Profile

Student Life

	First-time, first year (freshmen students)	Undergraduates
Percent of students who are from out of state		
Percent of men who join fraternities		
Percent of women who join sororities		
Percent who live in college-owned, operated or affiliated housing		
Percent who live off campus or commute		
Percent of students 25 years of age and older		

Activities Offered

Campus ministries		
Choral groups		
Concert band		
Dance		
Drama/theater		
Internatonal Student Organization		
Jazz band		
Literary magazine		
Marching band		
Model UN		
Musical Theater		
Opera		
Pep band		
Radio station		
Student government		
Student newspaper		
Student-run film society		
Symphony orchestra		
Television station		
Yearbook		

ROTC

	On Campus	At Cooperating Institution	Name of Cooperating Institution
Army ROTC is offered			
Naval ROTC is offered			
Air Force ROTC is offered			

Source: Common Data Set Initiative

Appendix B: School Profile

Appendix C   Student Metrics Profile Checklist

Appendix C: Student Metrics Profile

Student's Name

High School   Unweighted GPA   Weighted GPA

SAT Composite   SAT Reading/Writing   SAT Math   SAT Essay

SAT Subject Test   Score   SAT Subject Test   Score

ACT Composite   English   Reading   Math   Science   Writing

College/University

	25th Percentile	75th Percentile	Average
SAT Composite			
SAT Reading/Writing			
SAT Math			
SAT Essay			
ACT Composite			
ACT English			
ACT Math			
ACT Writing			

Average Unweighted GPA   Does the college/university superscore?

Average Weighted GPA   Yes   No

Appendix C allows one to compare a high school student's basic metrics to those of the freshman class at a college or university in which he or she has an interest. The data for the school may be found in Section C of the Common Data Set for the college or university of interest and usually at an individual school's website.

Appendix D: Info Sessions / Campus Tour / Interviews Checklist

Appendix D: Info Session / Campus Tour / Interviews

College/University

Street

City   State   Zip

Admissions Contact   Contact Phone

Admissions Office Email

Regional Admissions Counselor   Counselor's Phone

Regional Counselor's Email

Date of Campus Visit   Information Session   Yes   No

Campus Tour   Yes   No   Interview on Campus   Yes   No

High School Visit   Yes   No   Date of High School Visit

Regional Visit   Yes   No   Date of Regional Visit

Location of Regional Visit

Alumnus Interview   Yes   No

Name of Interviewer

Interviewer Phone   Interviewer Email

Notes

Appendix E: Advanced Standing Checklist

Appendix E: Advanced Standing Checklist

Student Name

College/University   Maximum Credits Allowed

Advanced Placement Test	Student Score	Score for Credit	Credit
Art History			
Biology			
Calculus (AB)			
Calculus (BC)			
Chemistry			
Chinese Language and Culture			
Comparative Government & Politics			
Computer Science A			
Computer Science Principles			
English Language & Composition			
English Literature & Composition			
Environmental Science			
European History			
French Language			
German Language			
Human Geography			
Italian Language and Culture			
Japanese Language and Culture			
Latin			
Macroeconomics			
Microeconomics			
Music Theory			
Physics 1: Algebra-based			
Physics 2: Algebra-based			
Physics C: Mechanics			
Physics C: Electricity and Magnetism			
Psychology			
Research (Second part of AP Capstone program)			
Seminar (First part of AP Capstone program)			
Spanish Language			
Spanish Literature			
Statistics			
Studio Art (2-D, 3-D, & Drawing)			
U.S. History			
U.S. Government & Politics			
World History			
Total Credits			

Appendix E: Advanced Standing Checklist

Student Name

College/University   Credits to Graduate

Advanced Placement Test	Credits	Credit for Course	Enroll in
Art History			
Biology			
Calculus (AB)			
Calculus (BC)			
Chemistry			
Chinese Language and Culture			
Comparative Government & Politics			
Computer Science A			
Computer Science Principles			
English Language & Composition			
English Literature & Composition			
Environmental Science			
European History			
French Language			
German Language			
Human Geography			
Italian Language and Culture			
Japanese Language and Culture			
Latin			
Macroeconomics			
Microeconomics			
Music Theory			
Physics 1: Algebra-based			
Physics 2: Algebra-based			
Physics C: Mechanics			
Physics C: Electricity and Magnetism			
Psychology			
Research (Second part of AP Capstone program)			
Seminar (First part of AP Capstone program)			
Spanish Language			
Spanish Literature			
Statistics			
Studio Art (2-D, 3-D, & Drawing)			
U.S. History			
U.S. Government & Politics			
World History			
Total Credits			

Appendix F: Admissions Timelines Checklist

Appendix F: Admissions Timelines Checklist

Student Name
College/University

Event	Deadline	Date Completed
Application - Early Action		
Application - Early Decision		
Notification of Early Admission		
Application - Regular Decision		
Notification of Regular Decision Admission		
Submission of Letters of Recommendation		
Submission of High School Transcript		
SAT Test Registration		
ACT Test Registration		
Latest Date by which SAT or ACT Tests must be submitted		
Latest Date by which SAT Subject Tests must be submitted		
AP Test Registration		
FAFSA Priority Date		
FAFSA Last Day to Submit Required Forms		
CSS / Financial Aid Profile		
Notification of Financial Aid Award		
Acceptance Reply Date with Deposit		
Transfer Application Deadline		
Housing Deposit		

Application Type Accepted	Yes	Date Completed
Common Application		
Universal Application		
Coalition Application		
School's Own Application		

	Yes	Date App Submitted
Rolling Admssion		

Appendix G: Financial Aid Checklist

Appendix G: Financial Aid Checklist

Student's Name

General Contact Information
Name of College/University
Mailing Address:
Mailing Address City/State/Zip/Country:
Street Address (if different):
Street Address City/State/Zip/Country:
Main Phone Number:
Toll-Free Phone Number
WWW Home Page Address:
Financial Aid Office Mailing Address:
Financial Aid City/State/Zip/Country:
Financial Aid Phone Number:
Financial Aid Fax Number:
Financial Aid E-mail Address:

Financial Aid Office Contact

Financial Aid Office Contact's Title

Notes

Appendix G: Financial Aid Checklist

Undergraduate Full Time Expenses		
	Freshman	Undergraduates
PRIVATE INSTITUTIONS Tuition:		
PUBLIC INSTITUTIONS Tuition: In-district		
PUBLIC INSTITUTIONS Tuition: In-state (out-of-district):		
PUBLIC INSTITUTIONS Tuition Out-of-state:		
NONRESIDENT ALIENS Tuition:		
REQUIRED FEES:		
ROOM AND BOARD: (on-campus)		
ROOM ONLY: (on-campus)		
BOARD ONLY: (on-campus meal plan)		
Comprehensive tuition and room and board fee (if college cannot provide separate tuition and room and board fees		

Estimated Expenses	Residents	Commuters (living at home)	Commuters (not living at home)
Books and supplies			
Room only			
Board only			
Room and board total (if your college cannot provide separate room and board figures for commuters not living at home):			
Transportation			
Other expenses			

Undergraduate per-credit-hour charges	Tuition Only
PRIVATE INSTITUTIONS	
PUBLIC INSTITUTIONS In-district:	
PUBLIC INSTITUTIONS In-state (out-of-district):	
PUBLIC INSTITUTIONS Out-of-state:	
NONRESIDENT ALIENS:	

Net Price Calculator	
Total Cost of Attendance	
Expected Famiy Contribution	
Estimated Financial Aid	

Appendix G: Financial Aid Checklist

Net Price Calculator Factors

Family Informaiton

Citizenship	
Primary State Residence	
Number of Children in College	
Number of People in Your Family	

Parental Income

Gross Wages/Salary	
Interest/Dividend Income	
Business/Farm Income	
Other Income	

Total Income	

Assets

Student Assets	

Parental Assets	
Cash and Investments	
Business/Farm equity	
Real Estate Equity (but not home equity)	
Other Assets	

Total Assets	

Total Billed and Unbilled Costs

Tuition and Fees	
Room and Board	
Estimated Personal Expenses (including books)	
Estimated Travel Costs	

Your Estimated Scholarship	

Expected Family Contribution	

Appendix G: Financial Aid Checklist

Financial Aid Forms first year domestic students' financial aid applications must submit

FAFSA	
Institution's own financial aid form	
CSS/Financial Aid Profile	
State aid form	
Noncustodial profile	
Business/farm supplement	
Other (specify)	

Filing Date for first year students

Priority date for filing required financial aid forms	
Deadline for filing required financial aid forms	
No deadline for filing required forms (applications processed on a rolling basis)	

Notification Dates for first year students)

Students notified on or about	
Students notified on a rolling basis	
Students must reply by or within _____ weeks of notification	

Criteria used in awarding institutional aid

	Non-need based	Need-based
Academics		
Alumni Affiliation		
Art		
Athletics		
Job Skills		
ROTC		
Leadership		
Minority Status		
Music/Drama		
Religious affiliation		
State/district residency		

Appendix G: Financial Aid Checklist

Types of Aid Available

Loans (CDS H12)

Federal Direct Student Loan Program	
Direct Subsidized Stafford Loans	
Direct Unsubsidized Stafford Loans	
Direct PLUS Loans	
Federal Perkins Loans	
Federal Nursing Loans	
State Loans	
College/university loans from institutional funds	
Other (specify)	

Scholarships and Grants

Need Based

Federal Pell	
SEOG	
State scholarships/grants	
Private scholarships	
College/university scholarship or grant aid from institutional funds	
United Negro College Fund	
Federal Nursing Scholarship	
Other (specify)	

Appendix G: Financial Aid Checklist

Number of Enrolled Students Awarded Aid	First Time Full Time Freshman
Number of degree seeking students	
Number of students who applied for need-based financial aid	
Number of students who were determined to have financial need	
Number of students who were awarded financial aid	
Number of students awarded financial aid who were awarded need-based scholarship or grant aid	
Number of students who were awarded any need-bsaed self-help aid	
Number of studnets who were awarded ny non-need-based scholarship or grant aid	
Number of students who were awarded financial aid who had need fully met (exclude PLUS loans, unsubsidized loans, and private alternative loans)	
Average financial aid package of those who were awarded financial aid. Exlclude any resources that were awarded to replace EFC (PLUS loans , unsubsidized loans, and private alternative loans)	
Average need-based scholarship and grant award of those awarded any need-based scholarship or grant aid	
Average need-based self-help award (excluding PLUS loans, unsubsidized loans, and private alternative loans)	
Average need-based loan (excluding PLUS loans, unsubsidized loans, and private alternative loans) of those students awarded need-based self-help aid who were awarded a need-based loan	

Number of Enrolled Students Awarded Non-Need Based Scholarships and Grants	First Time Full Time Freshman
Number of students who had no finacial need and who were awarded institutional non-need based scholarship or grant aid (exclude those who were awarded athletic awards and tuition benefits)	
Average dollar amount of institutional non-need based scholarship or grant aid	
Number of students awarded non-need aid who were awarded non-need-based athletic scholarships or grant aid	
Average dollar amount of institutional non-need based athletic scholarships or grant aid	

Source: Common Data Set Initiative: Sections G and H

Appendix G: Financial Aid Checklist

Appendix H: Admitting School Checklist

Appendix H: Admitting School Checklist
General Information

Name of College/University
Mailing Address:
City/State/Zip/Country:
Street Address (if different):
City/State/Zip/Country:
Main Phone Number:
WWW Home Page Address:
Admissions Phone Number:
Admissions Toll-Free Phone Number:
Admissions Office Mailing Address:
City/State/Zip/Country:
Admissions Fax Number:
Admissions E-mail Address:

Admitted Students Day	Start Date	Stop Date	Attending

Major Interest	Rank among Admitted Schools	
Tour Department	Meet with Faculty?	Rate Faculty (1-5)
Did you attend classes	Rate the Classes	Rate the Housing
Rate the food on campus	Rate the school's overall fit with what you want from your college experience	
Financial Aid Package	Expected Family Contribution	
Grants		
Loans		
Student Contribution		

Degrees Conferred Category

	% of Bachelor's
Agriculture	
Natural resources and conservation	
Architecture	
Area, ethnic, and gender studies	
Communication/journalism	
Communication technologies	
Computer and information sciences	
Personal and culinary services	
Education	
Engineering	
Engineering technologies	
Foreign languages, literatures, and linguistics	
Family and consumer sciences	
Law/legal studies	
English	
Liberal arts/general studies	
Library science	
Biological/life sciences	
Mathematics and statistics	
Military science and military technologies	
Interdisciplinary studies	
Parks and recreation	
Philosophy and religious studies	
Theology and religious vocations	
Physical sciences	
Science technologies	
Psychology	
Homeland Security, law enforcement, firefighting, and protective services	
Public administration and social services	
Social sciences	
Construction trades	
Mechanic and repair technologies	
Precision production	
Transportation and materials moving	
Visual and performing arts	
Health professions and related programs	
Business/marketing	
History	
Other	

Appendix I: Scholarship Checklist

Name of Scholarship	Grantor	Amount	Need Based	Start Date	Deadline	Type of Application	Website

Appendix I: Scholarship Checklist

Appendix J: Sample of Email Parents Shouldn't Send

Dear Director of Admission,

My daughter does not want me to interject between you and her, but as a parent who is concerned about her academic future and who is ultimately paying the bill for her education, I will not remain silent in view of your decision to defer her application to the Honors College. I think that you need to reconsider your decision. Obviously it is easy to dismiss my suggestion as the typical interference of a helicopter parent, but before you do, please consider the following:

- She is someone who has loved learning since she started Montessori at age 3.
- She has never had a grade of less than A in middle school, high school or college and this includes her enrollment in the Gifted Student Program at Michigan State University where she completed four years of high school English and Math in two years, both of which with an A+.
- She taught herself calculus between her sophomore and junior year and will have completed multivariable calculus and differential equations at Michigan State University by the time she graduates this spring. So far she has had perfect scores on her mid-terms and one final at MSU.

In addition to enrollment in the Gifted Student Program, she has completed five AP classes with scores of 4 and 5 and will have completed 8 classes by the time she graduates with an emphasis on STEM courses. As I understand U of M's AP Placement Credit Policy, between her courses at MSU and her AP classes she could have as many as 36 credits at U of M before she starts her first class. At present she has received the College Board's AP Scholar with Distinction Award and, if she continues to excel this year, will graduate with an AP National Scholar Award.

She has a score of 800 on her SAT Math 2 Subject Test and her SAT Biology Subject Test. Her SAT score of 1470 is within your College's median.

She is an active participant in her classes and I think if you review her teacher recommendations, my guess is that they will be very positive.

Academically she is one of her high school's standouts, though they do not rank their students or identify a Valedictorian or Salutatorian so I can't tell you where she stands academically relative to her classmates.

But she is much more than an academic standout. For four years she has been actively engaged in the High School Theater program. She had the lead in the fall drama as a sophomore and played Elle Woods in *Legally Blonde* in the spring musical her junior year. Her director and music teacher nominated her for the Ovation Award for her performance. This fall she had a female lead in *The Importance of Being Ernest* and has one of the two female leads in *Guys and Dolls* this winter.

Her extracurricular activities don't stop there. In addition to the normal ones like her membership in the National Honors Society, her contributions to the school paper and her participation in student government as an officer, she has taken an active role in promoting STEM for females not only in her local community but around the country.

Two years ago she founded a club, Students for Females in STEM (SFS). Her high school does not offer an in-class computer science course. SFS has attempted to make up for this deficiency by twice offering a community education event called Coding and Cookies where more than 150 families have participated in the international program, Hour of Code. The club largely under my daughter's leadership has formed a partnership with students from MSU who have taught computer science in an after school program at her high school and are currently providing an in-school instructional program teaching coding and computer science basics through a grant from Google.

She has become an advocate for expanded computer science education in K-12 schools in Michigan and across the country. She has been to the White House twice as part of the Computer Science Education Coalition where she met with staff from the Office of Science and Technology Policy, lobbied Senators on Capitol Hill in Washington, lobbied the Governors of Arkansas, Kentucky, and Iowa at the National Governors Association's Summer Conference in Des Moines Iowa on the importance of state support for computer science education, and made a presentation to the Michigan State Board of Education on the need for computer science education in Michigan's K-12 schools. She and three of her club members met with Governor Snyder this past summer and so impressed him with their seriousness, that he singled them out in his State of the State Address last month.

I have taught graduate students at the School of Social Work at Michigan State University and I can say without hesitation that my daughter is the sort of student I would have wanted in my classroom. She is an engaged and passionate student who thinks not only of herself but also of her fellow classmates. She has a genuine love of learning and values the teacher/student relationship which is why enrollment in the Honors College matters to her. She talked last week to a person who read her application to the Honors College and seems to think that one of the reasons she was deferred was because she didn't mention her interest in the Honors College in her original application to U of M. If this is true, it seems rather short sighted on your part.

I know as a parent who is concerned about the learning environment my daughter will encounter in college, I would have a difficult time supporting a decision to enroll at the University of Michigan without admission to the Honors College.

If you still have an interest in her as a student, I would suggest you review your decision to defer her application and let her know your final decision before she decides in early April where she will be attending college next fall.

Stuart White, PhD

Appendix K: Frequently Asked Questions

What chances do I have if I applied to an Ivy League or MIT university?

Ask yourself the following questions:

Are the courses I am taking rigorous? Do they include Honors, AP and college courses?

Do I have 4s and 5s on my AP Tests?

Am I in the top 5% of my class?

Am I in the 98th percentile or higher of SAT or ACT test takers?

Do I have a perfect or near perfect score on my SAT Subject Tests?

How do I show prospective schools that I love to learn?

Are my extracurricular activities focused enough to show that I excel at a few things that I am passionate about?

What can I do to give back to my community and people less fortunate than me?

Do I have any significant accomplishments or contributions on a state or national level?

How do I show that I can play nice in the sandbox with my peers?

Will my teachers and guidance counselor recommend me enthusiastically?

What do I want to show about myself in my essay and interview that is authentic and interesting?

And perhaps most importantly, why do I want to attend HYP or MIT that shows them I will add value to the school as a student?

Being an international student, what should I do in grade 10 to make my application stand out to MIT?

Find the solution to cold fusion. Reverse climate change. Create a sustainable food supply for an exploding global population. And after you have done all that end global poverty.

As a sophomore in high school, you should be focused on your personal development as a student, a friend, a member of a community, and a person with a passion for something that matters to you.

Even if your academics are impeccable, you still have a mountain to climb given your status as an international student. Only 3 out of 100 international applicants are accepted at MIT and most of these applicants are capable of doing the work at MIT if accepted.

So stay true to your own truth and pursue it with vigor. Give back to your community where you can and when time allows.

If you are a leader in your school in a club or activity that you originated, develop a succession plan for when you have moved on to college.

Develop an academic schedule for your junior and senior year that reflects what you want to learn, not what you think you need to have on a MIT worthy transcript. But keep in mind that the courses should be the most challenging your school offers in the subjects you pursue.

Prep for the standardized tests that you are required to submit with your application. Don't think that just because school is easy, the standardized tests will be a cakewalk. Only 32,000 test takers out of 1.6 million get a score of 34 or higher on the ACT.

And make sure you don't put all your eggs in one basket. There are incredible colleges and universities in the US that can meet your need for a technical education. Carnegie Mellon, the University of Michigan School of Engineering, University of Berkeley School of Engineering, the University of Illinois School of Engineering, Cal Tech, Georgia Tech, Harvey Mudd, the University of Austin, Northwestern School of Engineering, Purdue School of Engineering and even Michigan Tech come to mind.

What are my chances to get into top universities in the US for undergraduate programs?

Your academic achievement and test scores appear to be competitive for a top university. My one concern is that you have a laundry list of extracurricular activities that suggests resume building rather than a passionate pursuit of a few things at which you excel.

You will need to wrap up the list into a narrative about a person whom other students would want to spend time with and get to know. Think of your task as though you were a fly fisherman who is looking for the perfect hook that will snag the rainbow trout swimming through your favorite stream. The admission officers reviewing your application are the trout and the application process is your stream. Now find your hook.

What distinguishes you from the countless other international students who are qualified for admission to top schools in the US? And don't forget that for most of these schools the admission rate is between 3 and 5% of all applicants. So you need to be highly distinctive.

Generally, the qualities that elite schools are looking for that can be the basis of a hook are a:

- lifelong love of learning;
- highly evolved competency in one or two things that place you at a national level of achievement;
- commitment to your community outside your school with an eye toward what you are giving back to people less fortunate than yourself; and
- passion for excellence in your select activities.

You will need other people - teachers and people with whom you work who know you well - to reinforce the narrative you are trying to create for yourself.

Good luck on your journey. You are on the right track.

Should I apply to Harvard with a 3.7 GPA?

Here is a simple calculation you can do to see if you are competitive at a school like Harvard.

Take your SAT score if you took the SAT and add the Reading and Math scores together, divide by two and multiply by one tenth. This should give you a number between 70 and 80. If your SAT scores are less than 1400, you are below the 25th percentile for the school which is not good. Let's say the resulting number is 75.

Now take the two SAT Subject Test scores that Harvard wants and add them together, divide by two and multiply by one tenth. Let's say you had a 780 on Math and a 740 on Physics. The resulting number is 76.

Finally, your un-weighted GPA of 3.7 in a course load that has a sufficient number of AP, honors, and college courses to merit college prep level is equal to 71 according to Michele Hernández in her book *A is for Admission: The Insiders Guide to Getting into the Ivy League and Other Top Colleges.*

Your Academic Index is the sum of these three final numbers or 222. The top score you can receive is a 240. According to a report in the *New York Times* the average academic index of students admitted to Harvard, Princeton and Yale is 220. So yes, you have a chance to get in if you have a 1500 SAT score and near perfect SAT Subject Test scores along with a 3.7 GPA.

To calculate your Academic Index, go to The (Secret) Academic Index Calculator used by Ivy League Colleges.

Keep in mind your extra-curriculars and how you present yourself in writing and at your interview will play a role in whether you get into Harvard or not as well as your grades and test scores.

What does MIT look for when accepting students?

I've answered this question before so I will try to sum up what I think elite schools like MIT are looking for in applicants.

First, you must meet a minimum threshold of eligibility. This includes:

- a high GPA with a rigorous course load of AP, honors and even college courses;
- a score on the ACT or SAT that places you between the 25th and 75th percentile or higher among admitted students (you can check the student profile on MIT's web site to find this metric);
- near-perfect SAT Subject Tests with one test being Math; and
- a class ranking near the top of your class if your high school ranks students.

In combination, these metrics create leverage for your application. Leverage will open the door and get your application a second look.

But elite schools are interested in more than high performing students where academics and the capacity to do the work of a college student are concerned. They are looking for leadership potential and the prospect of adding value to the school.

In this regard, they will consider the depth of an applicant's commitment to something other than coursework. Did you start a nonprofit, develop a research project that merited publication, win a state or national award as an athlete, artist, or scientist? Do you have a passion for excellence or are your someone who has spread yourself thin in order to try to impress the admissions officials with your extra-curriculars? The latter are considered resume builders and don't fare well when the committee meets to review applications.

Do you have a love of learning that your teachers will confirm when they write your letters of recommendation? Are you one of the most exceptional students they have taught and will they commit this to print?

Are you a legacy or a first generation college student? These factors could help your application although in themselves they are not determinative.

Have you given back to your community beyond school in an effort to help others less fortunate than you? How deep is your commitment? Do you volunteer at your local hospital just so you can say you have volunteered somewhere or do you really want to contribute to your community's health and well being? Will someone attached to this activity back you up with a positive supplemental recommendation?

And then there is the narrative you create for yourself. Your essay will show the admissions office what you value the most about yourself. Be authentic and interesting. You want the person reading your essay and your responses to MIT's supplemental questions to finish with the impression that you are someone the reader wants to know more about, preferably as an admitted student.

And make certain that when you interview with a MIT alumnus, your oral narrative is consistent with your written one. Even though you will be nervous when you interview, don't forget to be as likable as you know how to be. Elite schools are looking for highly competent students who will work in a team atmosphere to build up their fellow students as well as themselves.

Finally, a factor some schools consider is demonstrated interest. Did you visit the school or meet with a school representative when they toured your state? Part of demonstrating interest is when you choose to apply. Early decision and early action applications tend to have a higher admission rate. For example, if you want to improve your chances of admission to MIT, then consider applying Early Action. In 2016, 8.4% of MIT's 7,767 early action applicants were admitted. Out of MIT's 16,029 regular decision applicants, only 5.1% were admitted.

In other words, your task is to show MIT what makes you stand out from the thousands of applicants who have the leverage required of admitted students. And don't be disappointed if after doing all of this, you end up on the short end of the straw. At the end of the day, MIT is a reach school for every applicant.

Can I get into a good college solely off a perfect SAT score?

No. Highly rated colleges and universities take a holistic approach to admissions. They are looking for two basic qualities in their applicants - leadership and leverage.

Leverage is made up of an applicant's GPA, standardized test score, class rank, coursework rigor, and for some schools SAT Subject Test scores. Your SAT score is just one variable among many that are considered. If you don't have the leverage to get the attention of the admissions officer looking at your application, your leadership qualities probably won't help you.

Top schools are looking for students who will add value to the school in the near term and the long term. What will you add to the admitted class? To answer this question they will look for evidence of love of learning as well as a commitment to something other than course work. Do your outside class activities show depth of purpose? Are you giving something back to your school or your community? Is there something unique about you that other students can benefit from?

Your essay response, your response to supplemental questions, your letters of recommendation will speak to your leadership activities as well as your character.

In other words, top colleges and universities are looking for a complete package and not just a feature. To be sure, you are already a special student if you have a perfect SAT score. Less than one tenth of one percent of the SAT test takers obtain a perfect score. You should be considered for a National Merit scholarship with this score. If you do qualify as a National Merit finalist, then you have gone a long way to demonstrating that you are a student who will add value to the school you attend. But make certain that the story you tell about yourself in your application affirms this as well.

ABOUT THE AUTHOR

In 1980, the Graduate Theological Union (GTU) in Berkeley awarded Dr. White a PhD in the interdisciplinary field of art and religion. His thesis was an original Passion Play titled *Martyr: a Passion in Three Acts*. Before completing his doctorate, he received a Masters of Divinity from the Church Divinity School of the Pacific, an Episcopal Seminary in Berkeley, California.

While he was a student at the GTU, Dr. White served on the admissions committee reviewing graduate school applications for his field. After graduation, Dr. White returned to his home state of Michigan and began working in the field of aging for 25 years. He has authored several notable reports on the state of human services in Michigan. For six years, Dr. White taught information technology to Masters of Social Work students at Michigan State University. Dr. White has three children. His first foray into helping his children with the college application process ended with his eldest daughter's enrollment in Yale University.

If the readers of the print or Kindle version of *College Admissions: A Parent's Guide* would like fillable PDF versions of the Appendices, they are available to download at www.collegeadmissions.guide.

www.ingramcontent.com/pod-product-compliance
Lightning Source LLC
Chambersburg PA
CBHW070522030426
42337CB00016B/2068